TRUSTING THE
INTELLIGENCE OF SPIRIT

REFLECTIONS ALONG THE PATHWAY OF MEDIUMSHIP - AN EXPERIENTIAL PERSPECTIVE

HELEN DAVITA DSNU

THE WRITER SPIRIT

EPIGRAPH

Spirit is that which sees the truth of each moment, and does not cling to any conclusion

———————————

INTRODUCTION

Look deep inside yourself. That's where the magical spirit intelligence is revealed. The more you look, the more you realise that your conscious mind isn't always in control. The moments of inspirational ideas, the 'gut' feelings that guide you from danger, that sense of already knowing a stranger, all live in the subconscious mind.

You are not alone. Deep inside your subconscious mind, your own spirit is working hard to give you guidance, wisdom, knowledge, and answers to important questions. Look deeper, stay there longer and the spirit intelligence from those both here and those who have gone before us, may be revealed.

We cannot pinpoint the subconscious mind in the human body. Nobody can locate the origin of a thought. It appears to be existential to the body and beyond our internal cellular network. It is without flesh (<u>discarnate</u>) and indestructible. After all, how can we cancel a thought that has arisen? We can't 'unthink' anything. The best we can do is to either forget it, change it, analyse it, enjoy it, share it, or ignore it - but it is out there somewhere and is beyond cancellation. It can be buried but never truly forgotten.

Many will come to know their 'gut feelings' as their intuition. Intuition also has fields of intelligence and an awareness beyond memories, consensus and associated experiences. It knows what to say and do. It knows beyond an earthly existence what is happening now in our physical world. It knows that life is spirit, that responds, reacts, knows the right time to reveal its presence and how best to achieve this.

Over my years as an evidential medium, an intuitive and a teacher, my quest has been attempting to explore, trust and understand spirit intelligence.

I have sought to define for my own needs any elusive boundary between intuition (psychic) and genuine afterlife communication (evidential). The psychic and evidential communications are so closely related that the differences may be confused or incorrectly attributed. I couldn't have continued my work honestly, if someone believed I had communicated with their deceased loved ones - when I didn't have that certainty myself. Giving false hope was never an option and a fear that the most genuinely motivated mediums I know, encounter.

The benchmark for many mediums is the 'presence of spirit.' The absence or presence of an 'atmospheric' power being the defining factor. This atmosphere feels charged with emotion. Many comment that when it is present, they feel goosebumps on the skin and a change in temperature. Others experience a sensation of cobwebs on the face.

However, it is just as possible to experience the signs of an atmosphere of 'presence' through intuition, by giving a tarot card reading. It is equally possible to experience the 'presence' during a hypnotherapy session. Could this 'presence of spirit' be a simple manifestation of emotion or a change of brain wave states? Are mediums manifesting something we 'call' intelligence when in reality, we have tapped into natural states of phenomena, through cause and effect?

My conclusions at this point, from my knowledge and experience, are that when we analyse from an experiential perspective, we require at least the sense of 'presence' - plus two major fields of spirit intelligence.

The first field of spirit intelligence is the emotional. This is where the spirit reveals an awareness of self and of others.

The second field of intelligence is social, and the spirit reveals a knowing of what to say, do, or both. I call this combination the emotional/social intelligence (ESi).

A brilliant teacher once said, "I don't care if it is psychic or evidential - it's all from the spirit," and my path has shown this to be true.

Could it be that when we communicate spiritually or intuitively, all the intelligence can be accessed within our subconscious - even that of our loved ones? Or perhaps there are multilayered fields of intelligence and we need to open doors to them in our minds.

I believe we may be as close as ever to finding these answers, if we analyse our spirit communications, with a recipe of ESi and the enigmatic presence of spirit.

I have both treasured and cursed this journey and hope that in reflecting on my experiences; you take from it my passion that the intelligence of spirit is authentic, tangible, amazing and the thrust to knowing our eternal nature.

As I journey through my ongoing quest for understanding the intelligence of spirit, I reveal real-life stories and communications from those living their next life.

PREFACE

On September 1st 2018, flight FR806, London Stansted to Knock West of Ireland - landed safely and delivered me home from the Arthur Findlay College for the last time.

Jackie was waiting for me in the car and helped me load my suitcases, bought me coffee at the local garage and drove the 15 minute journey back to our cottage in rural Ireland. A full week of teaching at the college always exhausted me, but this time it was different. I was seriously ill.

By the next evening I was in hospital, unable to breathe efficiently, because of an exacerbation of a long-standing lung disease.

It was time to take stock of my work life and make significant changes for the future. If I carried on as I had been, I could not survive.

My mind was still full of ideas and plans for work. My diary had 3 years of high ticket bookings on all continents of the world - to be fulfilled. Yet my body could no longer cope with the intense demands of international travel, adapting to different time zones, exhausting teaching weeks with long working hours, lonely sleepless nights in unfamiliar beds. The routine was just too physically punishing.

Within a few days of treatment, I was back at home and resting. Yet every time I felt an improvement and became more confident I could fulfil my work commitments, another health problem arose or my lung disease worsened.

Within a few months, my lungs were too weak. I also had a neurological condition which affected my balance, speech and coordination and an autoimmune disease, affecting my joints and mobility. These conditions were not new, they merely became so out of control and disabling that returning to my former schedule was impossible.

At the insistence of my wonderful friends and colleagues, the Arthur Findlay College coordinated with Spiritualist charities, to fund a garden buggy, so I could still get outside and enjoy the garden. Friends and former students in Australia were incredible, raising funds to help me purchase a mobility scooter. I felt valued and cared for, despite regular life being restricted and no working income anymore.

Also, the college promised that I could still teach online at the Arthur Findlay College, rather than travel there, and they would soon arrange this.

There was every hope I could put into reality all the new ideas, the experience and teaching skills I had enjoyed so much, and remain safe at home.

Bit by bit, we cancelled every work commitment, as at every attempt to return, my health failed me. I was by now reliant on a basic disability pension, but we managed by scaling down our lifestyle and focussing on what was important in life - quality, family, friends, our home, the animals and our happiness.

My last full course I organised at the college was on the emotional intelligence of the spirit and it was a fabulous course to end my physical teaching presence there.

Finding emotional intelligence with spirit was for our loved ones to express their self - awareness. Awareness of their loved ones and their uniqueness, within the evidence offered to a medium. It was to discover the point where a loved one can say without a doubt, it can only be them and nobody else. It was the cleverness of information that made it personal and specific and over the years; I had so many examples to share.

Emotionally intelligent evidence is the highlight of mental mediumship for the sitter - the 'wow' moments and the indisputable expression of the eternal spirit. The revelations of the beloved spirit people, assure their loved ones they have not gone forever and they can prove it!

However, we also find another area of intelligence that adds to the significance of compelling spirit communication and that is social intelligence.

Social intelligence is when we show positive expressions that reflect that we know the right thing to say and do. Our loved ones in spirit offer this to us and it makes a vast difference in awareness and belief of an afterlife. It bridges the fear that our loved ones who have passed are gone forever and reassures that they still understand what we need to know and what presently affects us.

I cannot think of a greater significance with evidential mediumship from our loved ones, than to share their emotional and social intelligence; so that we can really know they still thrive, they still love us, they still know us and still care about our lives.

There will be occasions when the intelligence of spirit becomes clear long after the communication and not during. In the moment of mediumship, this may appear frustrating and even cause doubts to creep in. As you read on, you see that trust in what you receive is vital and that holding back information, leads to missed opportunities for all concerned.

Now I write instead of flying. If the spirit can share their love so intelligently from heaven, then I can now share, in my own words, my experiences of their love and intelligence from the sanctuary of my home in Ireland.

As time moves forward, I reflect on the wonderful intelligence of spirit that I was honoured to experience, whilst analysing it with my critical mind. I treasure the journey I have taken and the path ahead, in the knowledge that this is an exciting, eternal quest.

The intelligence of spirit is truly life changing, once experienced.

In this book, I share some personal experiences where emotional and social intelligence (ESi) were present in communication from the spirit world. Nothing saddens me more than generic information from an inexperienced medium, being accepted by a recipient as proof. It's a poor excuse for the reality and beauty of intelligent truths from our spirit loved ones. As mediums we must strive to be the very best channel of communication, to deliver the eternal message of love. It is so much more than finding names, dates, occupations and hobbies. It is the power of love expressed beyond death.

We need to know whether the spirit lives on and is intelligent enough to express an eternal presence which makes sense to us. I believe the spirit offers intelligence in buckets - if we are truly prepared to receive and brave enough to trust.

All mediums will enter periods in their lives when they doubt their ability and the existence of the spirit world. Some will give up their work and start afresh. Others keep going until they rediscover the relevance and intelligence of communication.

I have not embellished, exaggerated or copied the authentic experiences in this book. They all happened on my watch as a medium. I hope that for all who doubt their path, or the proof of life after death, they read this account and reflect on their own truth and experiences, through their rational mind.

I do not seek to convince anyone who doesn't believe in life after death. I share with you my greatest respect for the intelligent, relevant communications of the loved ones we all miss from this world. I share the evidence of what I believe by their death, was a new journey of life, through their intelligent contact.

For balance, I include some events that were attributed to the intelligence of spirit, but actually were not. In these cases we can read how easy it is to believe that until we discover a rational explanation, not everything can be blamed on the discarnate spirit.

The authentic evidence for the intelligence of spirit can be overwhelming. They imprint all encounters with spirit upon the souls of those who were present. When the power and intelligence of spirit becomes your experience, a love and reverence for all life enriches you. This is the significant power of ESi.

This is not a book to showcase my ability as a medium. Like all professionals, I had my bad days too. It is a collection of experiences which show just how socially and emotionally intelligent we can all be now and beyond this physical life. It is an opportunity to discover the many ways we as incarnate and discarnate beings can communicate, creating significance and transformation in unexpected ways. It is also an opportunity for us to analyse and explore this intelligence and consider how to keep it central to mediumship development. It is part of the eternal dialogue.

My hope is that it encourages you to reflect on your own experiences of spirit intelligence, how beautiful it is, what you learned, what you shared and how it is intertwined with your personal soul development.

As you read through the wonders of spirit intelligence in this book, consider the ESi that is present in all mediumship communications. It is these aspects that leave us in no doubt that we are eternal. Our loved ones who have passed, are always thriving with the awareness and capacity to know what to do and say.

As I write from authentic personal experience, and my research with the phenomena that I have experienced. It is of no interest to me that something is thought to be true because it is written or said elsewhere. I could claim that my knowledge comes from a 'team' of afterlife educators, yet I know that should they be there encouraging me, they would expect that I reflect and work it out for myself. For this, I thank the spirit for crediting me with some intelligence too.

With a questioning mind and a former research background, I encourage all to question everything about these experiences and of course your own. That has always been my approach.

This is not a 'how to' book. It is a collection of experiences, exploring the nature of spirit intelligence within mediumship. I hope that each experience, gives you something to consider on your own path, that will help you and those you serve.

I could write of many theories and the fine words of respected pioneers and academics - ultimately you are your own pioneer on your own journey and will make up your own mind. For you are the intelligence of your own spirit.

After reading through the experiences and perspectives, I include a final chapter listing the advice I would give to my younger mediumship self, for nurturing the spirit intelligence in mediumship and personal development.

Our experiences as mediums will differ, and you may even disagree. Yet what truly matters is that you do your work honestly and simply facilitate the intelligence to take centre stage. If it's authentic, it will 'speak' for itself and our work as a 'broker' of communication completes.

I reference underlined terms in the glossary. I have changed names, and places to respect the identities of all involved, with the following experiences.

CONTENTS

_____

A POWERFUL ECHO

It was August 5th 2019, 12.45pm. Jackie sat at the dining table whilst I had a tray on my lap, as we both consumed soup and bread for lunch. The television was off and apart from the appreciative non specific murmurings of eating delicious food, everything else was quiet in the house and garden. That was until the Amazon 'echo dot' sprang into life loudly and spontaneously, playing 'Here Comes the Sun' by the Beatles. We both stopped eating and looked at each other in disbelief.

It was the song that was played at my brother's funeral earlier that year in March as we departed the crematorium. Jackie said to me, "do you think he's trying to let you know he's around still?" I replied I didn't know but as this was something that hadn't happened before, I was open-minded.

That was until the next song played and the next and the next.

Music played a huge part in my brother's life. He was a talented musician, a guitarist, a drummer and all his life he loved the Beatles. In later years, he played in a successful Beatles tribute band and also other local bands which played mostly 70's songs.

Music was such an important part of his life and a significant feature of his funeral. At the wake, his bandmates played several sets of songs live and the theatre group he was the sound engineer for, also sung live. I've never been to a funeral wake with so much live music.

His major career was in technology, as an executive analyst for IBM. After taking early retirement, he started a small business testing electrical compliance for companies. He also established himself as a 'sought after' theatre sound engineer, working with musical theatre groups. Plus his love of Beatles music and his bands is highly significant in our family.

Our little Amazon echo dot played the entire repertoire from his funeral and wake in the correct order, with no instruction from anywhere visible or audible. I did not have a copy of the playlist or order of the songs myself and most of the live music at the wake was spontaneous, rather than planned. Therefore, there was no chance anything in my emotional or physical possession could have triggered this event.

Eventually, after several songs and David Bowie's 'Starman' I had to ask Alexa to stop playing - it was too much and yes, my beautiful brother - you definitely made your intelligence known. As I gave the command to Alexa, I was aware of the powerful atmosphere in the room. It felt as if strong, loving arms had wrapped themselves around me. Jackie and I needed to take stock of what had just happened. Yet the only explanation was that his spirit intelligence knew the way to confirm his presence to us.

I had said after his passing that I did not want a medium to tell me they had his presence with them. I knew I'd be upset if they didn't do him justice. Many medium friends tried and failed, despite expressing my wishes not to go there. I was adamant I did not want to hear from him via a medium at his time. Despite the many years of bringing comfort to others this way, his passing was still too raw and personal to me for it to involve anyone who didn't know him.

The need to help a friend is strong during grief, so I was not angry with them - just frustrated by their lack of respecting my wishes. It served as a glorious reminder that we never give evidence of spirit unsolicited.

Their emails and messages fell upon my deaf ears, as I was clear that if there was a way to let me know he is fine, he would do it his way. He certainly did that day.

The 'emotional intelligence' my brother shared is the mutual awareness of relevant memorable music between us, the electronics and the technology. For me, it could have been no one else other than him.

It was touch and go, whether I would be well enough to attend his funeral. The playlist was mutual knowledge of that day.

He also showed what we know of as 'social intelligence' which is to either say or do what is appropriate. Music is a universal language that creates special bonds. It holds shared memories, takes us on journeys, tells us stories, defines eras, special events and has personality. The songs that played reassured me it could only have had his signature on them. He knew what to express and how to do it.

Looking back at over 35 years of mediumship as a professional, a teacher and course organiser at the Arthur Findlay College, nothing speaks louder from spirit than intelligence. It is the emotional and social relevance of that intelligence and the loving presence that makes it indisputable.

As we journey through this book, there are many beautiful souls who have shared their intelligence from behind the veil of eternal life and love. It is never as we expect and often has a deeper purpose - one they privilege us to share.

SAVING A SON'S LIFE

As I opened the front door to greet my sitter, it surprised me how physically strong he was. He was 6ft 5in and as 'ripped' as a bodybuilder. In a deep but gentle voice, he thanked me for agreeing to see him, and I led him into the lounge.

The sitting began with me explaining its purpose and what to expect. He had requested an evidential sitting, so I knew he wanted to hear from someone in the spirit world.

"No time to say goodbye" kept repeating clairaudiently in my mind. It is often my initial clue to hear a phrase, before the spirit draws closer and we can subsequently make a stronger evidential link. I mentioned that as I was making a connection, I had this information and my sitter smiled. I thought that this information alone was not enough and too generalised. Many of us know of someone who passed suddenly, so I was mentally busy welcoming the spirit in order to make a strong connection - so we could proceed.

I soon felt a powerful presence around me and as that built, my mind showed me a series of rapid images. I can only imagine it as being how some people describe of seeing their life flash before them!

I saw a man holding a baby, then watching the child play rugby. This man clutched his chest; the boy turned into my sitter and also an art exhibition of the paintings of Kandinsky! Kandinsky seemed out of place, but I trusted the process.

The ultimate image was of the man and my sitter in the car and with this, I heard the brakes screeching. As the images stopped, it felt as if his energy had moved through me and was continually flowing directly to my sitter. I was in this powerful stream and I was like an empty tunnel for his presence to reach what was now becoming obvious - his boy - his beloved son.

It was like a partially made jigsaw puzzle, so I set about making sense of it - adding the pieces together. I knew from the feeling of love I felt from my visiting spirit that this man was a father and from the love that flowed through me it was his dad, and I explained this. My sitter confirmed.

The rugby connection seemed obvious given the physique of my sitter, but I couldn't make that assumption. It had to be something more solid than the fact he was strong and muscular. I mentioned the rugby and my sitter confirmed with an affirmative, but I needed more, so I asked his dad to be more specific about the rugby connection. Almost instantly, I saw three lions running away. "England" I said to my sitter - you played for England" - but I was met with an answer I didn't expect. He said yes and no. Back to dad now and he showed me a damaged knee.

The information that we receive from the spirit world is never actually communicated in human language. The mind may translate into words and ideas but with no physical body, it is a thought consciousness speaking and we as mediums are the translators of thought forms. Therefore, images, symbols, sounds, and feelings from spirit are not always literal and as mediums we have to interpret them.

By now my mind was making more sense of the evidence and I stated he had played for England and now had an injury, which ruled him out of the team. As I saw this, another image from dad showed me him training the rugby teams. I explained this and that he was now coaching. He agreed. Phew!

I couldn't make any further sense of the art exhibition other than to state it. The response was very interesting. My international rugby coach was an art lover and had been to the Tate Modern gallery's Kandinsky exhibition recently. Apart from a love of art, he explained it inspired him to think in terms of patterns, colours, dynamics and that the artwork of Kandinsky inspired him in training the players tactically. His approach fascinated me and after the sitting we enjoyed a conversation about the energy of colours, patterns and symbols.

Last, I came to the aspect of the car journey with them both and the screeching brakes. I kept asking for more but was shown this image exactly as it was. Once I described this to my sitter, he became very emotional, and I allowed him to explain. Normally I just require validation of information (yes or no), but sometimes all you can do is pass on the information and hope it makes sense.

He explained that this was the reason he came to me. The incident had been so extraordinary to him, that unless there was another way to assure him it was real, he would conclude he was imagining it - yet never be satisfied with that explanation. He would always wonder.

On one night after rugby training, my sitter was driving home. His dad had been in spirit for a few months by then. He was approaching a road junction with traffic lights. The lights were green, so he knew to continue. However, he sensed a presence in the car and a human shape in the corner of his eye. When he looked across at the passenger seat, his deceased father was 'physically' there, sitting with him. It was such a shock that he slammed the brake pedal and came to a halt just before the junction. The lights were still green, but what happened next shook him to the core. A speeding oil tanker crossed his path at the moment his car had stopped (clearly having gone through a red light from the other direction). Had he not stopped at that moment, his car would have been hit at high speed. His father's spirit had just saved his life!

I thanked his dad in my mind and as I did so I saw his face, smiling and so beautiful - so I described the details of this to my sitter.

This wonderful hero of a father not only saved his son's life, but had the emotional and social intelligence to know what to say, how much to say, and what to leave for an explanation. Apart from his evidential intelligence, he also knew his son had to talk about this incident with someone who would believe him.

While the power of spirit flows through us, their intelligence may show visual phenomena, guiding us to accept their presence. For many, it is a case that they will only believe it is true, if it is something they can see with their own eyes.

As experienced by the rugby coach, spirit intelligence didn't disappoint. Because his deceased father was seen in the car, he would have most likely have died in a car crash otherwise. Such a powerful and emotional vision produced the intelligence to protect his much-loved son by shocking him into stopping the car.

Adding to this intelligence, was that his father must have had precognitive information of what was about to occur. With the oil tanker speeding through the red light - across his son's path, it would suggest that his father was 'looking out' for him from beyond this world.

The vision in the car led the son to seek an appointment with me. His father's knowledge of recent events (such as his visit to Tate Modern), also comforted him greatly and showed emotional intelligence - the awareness of recent events that were important to him.

Many have witnessed the physical apparition of a deceased loved one. It is often explained as a psychological aberration related to intense grief. However, in this case it would be hard to explain it as this, with so much at stake. Had the lights been red that night, we could consider that his brain had registered this, and the apparition was a safety mechanism. However, they were green. Without his father in spirit, we would never have met.

3

WE NEED TO DISCERN THE GENUINE INTELLIGENCE OF SPIRIT

If we are to offer mediumship, attempting to do anything other than serve the intelligence of spirit would be pointless. For all is spirit intelligence whether, thoughts, animal, mineral, plant or water - living in this world or beyond. It is the context, and those involved that understand why it is so intelligent.

Mediumship has been with us for thousands of years and the responsibility is still as great as it ever has been. We know that the ancient Greeks consulted the Oracles at Delphi. Other cultures consulted gods and spirits of the natural elements and many indigenous beliefs are based upon knowledge derived from animal spirit wisdom, herbal influences and ancestral tribal communications, in altered states of awareness.

Evolving religions and political powers have influenced opinions on the intention of spirit communication and a common narrative is that it is fraudulent or evil.

Scepticism of spirit communication is widespread. Many give their uninvited opinions. In an age when seeing is believing and modern scientific analysis is the benchmark for authenticity, it is easy to understand why people do not believe spirit communication is possible or relevant. Add to this that many don't feel mediumship is necessary when they grieve, whilst others would find it overwhelming, some may express disdain, disbelief, disapproval or simply have no interest.

Over the years some mediums have been 'exposed' as fraudsters and this has served a negative general opinion, despite the honesty and integrity of so many. The cruelty of genuine mediums being told they are preying on the vulnerable hurts. There is injustice as in all areas of life, there are cheats - but mediums take the brunt of it as a generalisation.

We should respect the different perspectives and consider why their views matter and if they have any merit. To study spirit communication through the mind of a sceptic is healthy. We need comparisons and critics for us to decide if what we do is right, authentic, and helpful. We need to question and what sets us apart intelligently, is the fact that mediums need to be convinced too. Not just a believer, or a wishful thinker, but convinced through total honesty, intellect, knowledge and integrity with the only conclusions we should reach - that the intelligence has come from the spirit.

From another perspective, imagine being in the spirit world and finding an opportunity to contact a loved one - yet nobody is listening to you. That must be so frustrating. Or imagine you foresee an urgent situation and you need to be heard or seen to make a difference.

I wonder about the process that without a medium being present, the father of the rugby coach appeared to him in the car and saved his life? Do we really need mediums, when spirit are capable of doing a great job without us? There is definitely a place for mediumship communication, without the intermediary of the spirit medium. These are intelligent questions we need an answer to and must ask both ourselves and the spirit.

Evaluating this specific incident, we could hypothesise different explanations, yet none of them could account for the presence and the emotional and social intelligence in that moment. For example, could the mind experience a precognitive event of the looming fuel tanker about to cross his path? Would he know in that moment that the one thing that would shock him into slamming on the brakes would be an apparition of his father? Also, could the subconscious mind have known that his instinctive reaction would have been to brake hard, instead of continue? Could all this have been so rapidly orchestrated through the mind defying the laws of time? It appears improbable.

Personally, so much is improbable in my mediumistic experiences, that you have to be there to believe it. Yet it is this process of my mind, to find out if what happens in mediumship is genuinely spirit intelligence. Or whether it originates from the spirit mind of the medium, or the spirit mind of someone who has passed on. On balance, a simpler explanation from the intelligence shown, directs my thoughts to explore the nature of evidential mediumship.

True evidential mediumship is a collaboration which deserves respect for the spirit of loved one's past, those who miss them, the medium and the knowledge of the power of the mind. For it to have value in our lives, we must express their intelligence and presence and offer this opportunity to the magic of mediumship. We must analyse and question too.

It is quite normal to doubt. Spirit intelligence doesn't require us to advocate on its behalf. We do this willingly and nobody from the spirit world interviewed or tested any mediums for the role they play in life. We chose this path ourselves and we disappoint nobody of consequence if we change direction.

When we recognise a common spiritual thread of enquiry with others, mediumship becomes extremely interesting, collaborative, shared and quite normal.

4

PHYSICAL PHENOMENA FROM THE SKY

For many spiritual seekers, physical mediumship is the 'Holy Grail' of evidence. Not only is it witnessed by all present, it is experienced through the human senses. For some, this makes it tangible and more relatable.

To sit in a room with people who all experience the same phenomena is a powerful endorsement of an 'other worldly' experience. It is always the intelligence that matters and has true significance for us. An object levitating, or the hearing of a discarnate voice, is something a skilled mentalist can achieve and yet still not claim it as an afterlife experience.

In mental mediumship, information given through a third party, such a medium, may be subject to suspicions and doubts. In my own experiences of mental mediumship sittings at home, I only ever requested the first name or pseudonym of my sitters (unless they were personal friends), yet sceptics would have us believe that the information must have been 'googled' if we are too accurate. We will never silence the doubters, but if we refer to the case of the rugby coach - he hadn't told a soul about his experiences. This was out of the fear he wouldn't be believed and he would suffer ridicule. His experience was far too precious to him for anyone to undermine it, disparage or question him.

Mental mediumship requires the emotional and social intelligence from spirit to be experienced beyond doubt. I wouldn't wish it to be any other way and who could blame anyone for being sceptical, if what they experienced was generic information that most of us could relate to. Factor in the grieving sitter desperate for proof a loved one in spirit is ok, who accepts everything the medium says, and then you can easily understand why there is scepticism.

When physical mediumship is genuine, it is remarkable. I have witnessed it - but it is very rare. I have also been central to the focus of phenomena frequently, when I have demonstrated for students. On these occasions, the intention was to sit for trance mediumship.

As the trance demonstrations progressed, physical phenomena such as transfiguration and balls of light moving around the room were witnessed by all present. It is not something I ever intended, or wished to develop further. I am content that whatever occurred was spontaneous and appropriate at that moment in time.

I believe that the intelligence of spirit can bring both physical and mental mediumship together and have experienced both in private sittings.

On a sunny afternoon in West London, my sitter arrived in good time for her appointment with me. I opened the door to greet her and was shocked by her appearance. She was visibly shaking, and tears rolled down her cheeks. I asked her what was the matter, and she told me she was so nervous. She had never seen a medium before and she thought it might be scary.

This was unusual. Although some appear a little nervous, perhaps even wary, I had never experienced such intense emotion and fear just before a sitting! I explained there was nothing to worry about and she was under no obligation to have the sitting, but if she would like to come in, she can sit down, ask me questions and just take a few moments to relax. During the usual small talk, she revealed she had actually driven for over 3 hours to see me. She was determined I could not know of her locally, and all I knew was her first name. It would have been a shame to have driven so far and not to complete the sitting.

I was determined to help her relax and made a joke. "Don't worry, it's not like the movies with booming thunder and the crack of lightning" and with that, right on cue was a massive thunderclap and the room lit with sheet lightning! You couldn't have timed it better if you were into special effects! We looked at each other and both simultaneously burst out laughing. From that point onwards, the sitting progressed. I would like to think it was the intelligence of spirit that created this weather event, but I can't rule out a one in a billion chance of it being a coincidence.

As the sitting began, I clairvoyantly saw a man and sensed their love for each other. The sitting continued with much spirit intelligence. I knew of their love but every time I tried to find more evidence - I was clairvoyantly shown a car park barrier coming down. Later she explained he was her childhood sweetheart and before he passed, they had rekindled contact and fell in love again, despite them both being married to someone else.

Because she had been so nervous, I didn't keep to time. One aspect of evidence from this man was that he worked with electrical cables and connections. I couldn't say he was an electrician, but he showed me images in my mind of cables, ladders, and electrical tools. Perhaps the electrical storm was actually a clue? However, after a significant amount of time, his loving presence and the intelligent evidence from this man in spirit - my connection was getting weaker. It was time to conclude.

As I explained to her, it was time to bring the communication to a close. My sitter asked me if I could just get one more thing from him. She believed he had genuinely communicated, but was there just one more thing he could say to prove it really was him?

With that question, the Sky tv remote on my coffee table flipped into the air about 5 feet and landed in her lap! It transpired after she recovered from the shock that he had been a Sky TV installer!

With his presence and evidence, I believe he manifested physical phenomena as an intelligent sign of his identity. The phenomena answered her question accurately. On my coffee table were several tv remotes, yet it was the Sky remote that came to her physically.

There is a physical phenomenon that is known as telekinesis, where energy from the mind is said to move or levitate objects. It's a theory and some experiments would suggest it is possible. I remember some years ago watching a television programme on Russian experiments with telekinesis, where a man supposedly moved a matchbook across a table, with the power of thought alone. We know the mind is a powerhouse of energy and the full potential unknown.

Yet we cannot always say that this is the rational explanation without fully controlled testing. Also, even without fully controlled testing, when it occurs spontaneously, we also cannot claim it must be telekineses too.

The logical intelligence of what happened throughout the whole sitting would suggest there was an element of intelligent physical and mental mediumship. Whatever the explanation, the spirit in question found a brilliant method for confirming himself to us.

If seeing is believing, then we may look to physical events in mediumship as an area of interest. We define physical mediumship as a physical event witnessed simultaneously by all present, relating to

the afterlife. It can occur within mental mediumship sittings too.

5

ETHERIC BLUEPRINT

The witnessing of the physical spirit phenomena is elusive and often unexpected when it occurs. There are several hypothetical reasons for this, and the common theme appears to be with manifesting the right physical, mental, emotional and spiritual conditions.

Once experienced, the quest begins in replicating the conditions and this is possibly why the séance room became so popular in the late 19th and early to mid-20th century. This was mainly because of modern Spiritualism emerging from events in Hydesville, USA in 1848.

On March 31st, 1848 in Hydesville, the young sisters Kate and Margareta Fox, responded to inexplicable knocking sounds in their bedroom and received what they reported as intelligent responses.

They created a code based upon the alphabet and are reported to have discovered the story of a murdered pedlar because of this communication code. The knocks were known as 'rappings' and the story of two girls soon spread, sparking a renewed interest in spirit communication.

Seances developed rapidly and were and still are dedicated to spirit communication. There are many seances today, but their popularity was once greater, when the Spiritualist movement later emerged, after the Hydesville rappings.

Seances comprise of small groups of people known as 'circles' who meet regularly throughout the world, in their homes. Some meet in darkened rooms, as it was thought that light would affect production of a material called ectoplasm. This 'ectoplasm' forms a visible living energy force which animates into functional parts such as eyes and hands and is alleged to be a vehicle for spirits to communicate. It may also create full forms of humans and animals and levitate objects amongst various other reported phenomena. Other seances meet in normal overhead room lighting or natural daylight.

Photographic evidence of ectoplasm appears to show a cloudy, light coloured material which varies in states, from gaseous to an evolving solid 'cotton wool' appearance. Often reported is an accompanying presence of an unpleasant organic scent. The source of the ectoplasm purportedly originates from a spirit medium's orifice and when analysed, reports have stated ectoplasm contains bodily cells, natural chemical elements, fibres, dyes and matter from the seance room itself.

At the end of the seance it is also believed that the ectoplasm returns to the medium's body and presumably all the non-human additions from the seance room, to their origins.

The question of the intelligence arises frequently within physical phenomena. When we consider ESi–we may emotionally relate it to relevant awareness of both the spirit world and the sitters present at a séance, if the phenomena relates to someone known in the spirit world communicating with at least one of the sitters.

Also, with social intelligence, we can ask ourselves: is the phenomena expressing itself appropriately, for the sitters needs?

Physical mediumship is mired in controversy and it is a case of you decide if it is relevant, intelligent and genuine for yourself. To be genuine, many believe that everyone should witness the same phenomena, because it is existential to the mind of the medium and should not be influenced by their subconscious.

What fascinates me is this existential aspect of a visible spiritual substance known as ectoplasm. Could there be alternative explanations for manifesting an intelligent spiritual substance, existential to the human body too? Does it have to originate in the human body, or can it materialise by itself from what materials are present in a room? Why do we need a mixture? Nobody really knows as it is so rare to experience it and test its true substance. Spiritualist history is full of witness accounts and perpetuates the little knowledge we have about ectoplasm.

In 2001, I lived in a large, Victorian terraced house in south Birmingham, UK. The house had a cheery atmosphere, and those who visited often commented on how lovely and relaxing it was. Yet whilst living there, I did experience significant physical phenomena frequently.

One night as I slept, I awoke in the early hours of the morning and experienced what sounds similar to sleep paralysis. This is a recognised experience where the brain and body haven't synced to each other before there is full wakefulness. Usually we wake up and move, stretch, turn over, etc. In sleep paralysis, your mind is awake, but your body is paralysed for a few moments until the two synchronise. It can last a few seconds, yet it can cause considerable concern in that short time. It is a confusing condition at the time it occurs and reassuringly it passes quickly.

On that occasion when it happened to me, I was lying on my back, woke up, opened my eyes, yet couldn't move! I didn't panic but in the bedroom's twilight, above me floated a perfectly formed blue mist, full length duplicate of my body–approximately 3 feet above me. I looked at it carefully (as that was about all I could do at that point) and it undulated a little, as if a breeze was moving it. Next, I could move my foot and in that moment, the misty form disappeared by rapidly descending back into my physical body.

After a few moments of thinking about what just happened, I drifted back to sleep and awoke hours later to hear my 4-year-old son knocking on the bedroom door.

By late morning and with some time to reflect, I researched as much as I could. I already knew about astral projection (where in theory we have a spiritual energy body, which can separate and travel to other places whilst we sleep). There are other theories too, such as the aura expanding. Or was this the mysterious and elusive ectoplasm?

As I considered all options, it made sense to me that what I experienced was myself witnessing my etheric blueprint–the whole of me being expressed beyond the physical body. Perhaps all the possibilities are the same (astral blueprint or ectoplasm). For me, the blueprint was right. Naturally, my thoughts turned to why it happened. What was the point of me experiencing this? Was I meant to do anything about it? Where was the intelligence?

There are no certain answers, but deep in my soul I felt I was meant to witness this to reassure me I am more than just a finite physical body. I had actually witnessed my spirit body double that exists beyond me physically. I'm satisfied that this was the intelligence of the experience. It was my spirit intelligence validating itself back to me as a human - a mirror.

Perhaps the etheric blueprint and ectoplasm are the same thing. Maybe the intelligence of me witnessing it was to let me know I had a capacity for physical mediumship. Or possibly, we all can have a similar experience if the conditions are right. We will never know for certain, and that's the beauty of it. It just is. Finding similar experiences and what they could mean to others came several years later.

6

THE BLUE IN THE BLUEPRINT

Around 2008, I was living in a small maisonette in Great Missenden, Buckinghamshire. My long-term relationship had broken down and with my son at the local school, I would conduct my private sittings during the day here, when I wasn't away teaching at the Arthur Findlay College.

On a beautiful sunny afternoon, I greeted my sitter and asked him to come upstairs to my sitting room. He appeared to be a regular good-looking young man of around 30, dressed in expensive trainers, designer jeans and T-shirt. He beamed a beautiful smile, and I ushered him to the sofa as I took my chair by the window. After exchanging a few pleasantries, I explained how I could work with him and also asked what he was hoping for from his appointment. It was clear it was an evidential sitting with intelligence of the spirit world.

I took a few breaths and was aware my energy was first connected to him. This happened automatically, although it is a good way to begin - as suddenly announcing a loved one is present could be shocking. Better to ease into it.

Three images flashed through my mind. One was of a very well know person, another of my father's old police helmet and the last image showed him in a hospice with another lady either side of a bed.

I mentioned to him a connection to the police and this certain well-known person. As I did this, my mind revealed an image of him with a gun and holster under his jacket. I explained he must be a protection officer or work in high level security. This was all confirmed, and I asked if he was ready to see who could contact him from the spirit world. He was, and we began.

Immediately I was back at the hospice scene. He was at the bedside of his mother, who was passing over soon, and on the other side of the bed was his aunt. This was confirmed, but what happened next stunned me. With no interpretation of images, I heard his mother say to me "I kept my promise and showed him I was on my way." I relayed this information, and it was accepted.

I needed more from his mother as that information alone was too general and when someone is getting ready to pass, many signs are attributed to the event by the grieving, such as birds or butterflies appearing, songs on the radio. What I was then shown was his mother in the bed sleeping and approximately 3 feet above her was the same type of etheric blueprint I had seen of myself in Birmingham a few years earlier.

I explained this event to him, and he agreed. The sitting continued for another half an hour and it then naturally concluded.

My protection officer looked happy but exhausted, so I said I was going to make a quick coffee for us both so he could take it all in before driving home. As we enjoyed the coffee and some chat, he explained some more.

His mother did pass in a hospice from cancer. He was an only child and his father had left when he was a small boy. So for most of his life, it was just the two of them as a family. His mother had one sister - his aunt and the two most significant people in her life were with her at the end of this part of the journey, on either side of her bed.

Before she went into the hospice she told her son, I will show you a sign when I'm on my way to heaven and it will mean that everything is fine. Two hours before she passed, her son witnessed the etheric blueprint floating above her. He turned to his aunt and said "she's gone now." But the aunt wouldn't believe it, as his mother continued to breathe strongly for another two hours. He let the subject drop, but quietly spoke to mum in his mind, as he watched her etheric blueprint float up to the ceiling and disappear. For the rest of the time, he comforted his aunt and held the hand of his mother's frail body, until her breath finally stopped two hours later.

He told me that until this happened he would never have believed in life after death, or even mediumship for that matter. His mother's spirit intelligence made itself aware in advance and returned to validate this. Somehow, his mother knew she could prepare him for her passing. She knew the right thing to say and do, and she delivered her promise from her spirit.

During the whole of the sitting, we felt the emotional power and presence in the room and as a lovely extra - we both noticed her perfume around us.

On March 16th 2011, my father passed into spirit in the late morning. My son was by now 13 years old and was at school that day. After receiving the news, it preoccupied my mind about telling my son sensitively. Particularly as they had a special bond, and it was his first experience of a family member passing.

Time seemed to pass slowly, but when I saw him walking up the drive to the house, my heart was in my mouth. I had to stop him from grunting hello and then running upstairs to play on his games console. Instead, as soon as he came through the door, he was telling me to sit down as he had something to tell me! This wasn't going to plan, but I thought I'd hear him out and then break the news about his grandpa.

It transpired that a few minutes after his grandfather had passed, my son was having his morning break, when a large flash of bright blue light passed over both his hands. It was so obvious that even his friends noticed it, were spooked by it, yet were amazed. They couldn't explain it and all day it was a talking point.

I gently broke the news about my father and naturally there was sadness, but my son to this day knows that his grandpa said goodbye to him just after he had passed away, with the appearance of his blueprint. The intelligence of this awareness brought great comfort to my son, who still talks about the 'blue light flash' and how his grandpa came back to him from the spirit.

Signs in the moments of passing over are treasured, intelligent communications we never forget.

7

GENERALISATIONS AND THE FRAUDS

Every professional medium working with integrity, is anxious about their field of work, because generalists or frauds also represent it.

By generalists, I refer to those who rely on generic, non-specific information, which is delivered as purporting to be spirit communication. People who work this way may believe they are working with an authentic spirit of intelligence. The majority are working with random thoughts from their own minds, or cliches which many relate to.

An example would be a medium who may express something similar to:

"I have a lady here in the spirit world who loved flowers and sends her love. Who understands this?"

Many understand this information. It is general and unrelated to spirit communication. The medium probably hasn't a genuine connection with a discarnate spirit, or if they have, they are not working together.

In reality, generalists haven't understood the power of their own mind and the sovereign intelligence of the discarnate spirit. Nor how to work together as a team. For those generalists, it is only fair to mention that in most cases, more education and personal development is the solution.

Knowing the power of your own spirit is the key to everything in mediumship. Racing ahead, without your power, is missing the point of your purpose in life - which is to express your magnificence of spirit in the universe. How can we truly empathise with spirit communication without this realisation? It takes one to know one.

There are many who take the path of mediumship before they are ready to work with the public. Some are encouraged to work too soon, by inexperienced or over enthusiastic teachers. We need to support them all as they find courage to know when they are ready, rather than rush them with the responsibility. Others may be deluded about their ability as a medium and won't listen to sound advice. We all have an individual path of learning our lessons, but responsibility is essential, as we are dealing with the emotions of life and death.

We know a couple of identifiable areas to describe tricks and techniques that masquerade as mediumship as cold reading and hot reading. Many mediums who can genuinely communicate spirit intelligence may also 'fall' into a pattern of cold reading, or weave a combination of both. Sceptics may also use the cold reading techniques to feign mediumship and subsequently reveal their techniques to discredit spirit communication. Done well, it appears plausible.

We base cold reading around the principle of cause and effect regarding responses. As a simple example:

Medium: "I have a lady with me who is in spirit - has your mother passed?"

Recipient: "yes"

Medium: "I feel this is your mother"

If affirmative the medium continues, gleaning information from the responses offered.

If the answer had been 'no' then the medium would adapt and possibly state it was a grandmother (pretty safe bet if the sitter is an adult) adding that they sensed a maternal link, anyway. Cold reading is based upon adapting the information given, from the responses or even body language received. Some mediums subconsciously conduct the cold reading technique and have no realisation they are doing so.

Some years ago I assessed a medium's ability for private readings, who didn't realise he was subconsciously cold reading. When it was pointed out, he was deeply upset and disappointed. However, it gave him an opportunity to look closely at his mediumship and spirit communication and make progress with further study and development.

Hot reading is when the medium has used information they already know about the recipient and subsequently presents it as mediumistic.

The frauds merely cheat - it's that simple!

Many of us and our critics may have witnessed generalisation and fraud disguised as mediumship. It devalues mediumship, fuels the sceptics, and damages morale. The authentic intelligence of spirit is so incredible that there really is no need for it. The serious professional will analyse their work, know the power of the influence of their own mind and identify what needs further development.

Sadly, for those unaware of working below par, they may never experience and appreciate the beauty of spirit intelligence.

Through a genuine mediumistic connection to spiritual consciousness, we understand the power of goodness, love and eternal wisdom. All this is unfulfilled by fraud and overlooked with generalisations.

A counter argument to poor mediumship has been that it is a choice if people want to waste their time or money. This is unethical and against moral and legal standards to charge for a service, knowing it will not be delivered. Even offered freely, it is morally wrong and cruel to deceive someone into believing their loved ones are communicating.

Such is the public concern about genuine mediumship, that some sitters attempt to test the medium's integrity. It's understandable that a belief that a loved one has just communicated with intelligence from beyond death could cause doubts later. Testing the medium fuels this need.

At my studio in West Sussex, a woman booked an evidential sitting with me. She wanted to know if there was any communication from her loved ones who had passed over. Everything went well, and she appeared satisfied. Before she left, she asked a question. "Can you tell me if my sister will ever find love?" It was a psychic question, but I relaxed back in my seat and took a moment to explore this.

Clairaudiently I heard "she already had" so I relayed this to the sitter and the sister confirmed she was in a happy relationship with a man she loved. She apologised for testing me and expressed that she wanted to believe that everything was true about her sitting, but was scared in case she had been clinging to false hope. I didn't mind this, although I was left with a sad feeling that the genuine workers are 'mopping up' the damage frauds have created.

The challenge, on a conscious or subconscious level, would be the assumption that her sister had not found her love. For a generalist or cold reader, the opportunity is tempting to imagine the outcome, rather than communicate at the level of the spirit.

On another occasion, after a lovely sitting with plenty of spirit intelligence, a different sitter asked me if her father (in spirit) saw all the flowers she arranged at his graveside? Again I took a moment and, clairvoyantly, saw a grave with no flowers. I felt I was about to disappoint her if she had gone to so much trouble with these flowers, but I had to be honest. As I explained I couldn't see any, she smiled and said "thank you for that." Her family were devout Jews and in their tradition, flowers were not a part of the funeral. It was another test, but I would rather the sitter had confidence with the intelligence of spirit, then leave with doubts in their mind.

In all walks of life, we have frauds. Sadly, in mediumship it is a term that has a mostly unfair association. Most mediums I have met, worked with and even taught are not frauds. They are dedicated to their work and are inspired to help others find significance, comfort and wisdom from mediumship.

Frauds exist in mediumship. Fraudulence is not mediumship and real mediumship is not fraud. However, it is possible to be both a medium and fraudulent. It is sad for me to admit I have witnessed this frequently.

Excuses aside, there may be reasons a genuine medium would cheat. First, if the medium's reputation is excellent, and they are having a bad day, there is a pressure to perform well and it may not be possible at the time. Second, every time a medium steps onto a platform to demonstrate their craft, they are under immense public pressure. Fear of failure in public and private is real, and every medium experiences this at some point. It is unacceptable to cheat, but important to realise why it occurs.

Honesty is important in all instances of mediumship. Most of us would rather a medium stated they didn't have a link and reschedule, or if in public end their demonstration early. It's not so easy when the expectation is upon you and you feel you are letting people down. For some sitters, they may have travelled a great distance to see you, taken time off work and built up so much hope that the medium can help them. We need to accept that there are reasons and we need to be understanding when a medium cannot work.

When a respected medium cheats and is 'found out' it hurts the field of mediumship greatly. Some may believe that if those who are considered respected are frauds, all the rest are too. We just need an honest, human approach and not assume all are frauds - even when it will cause disappointment. Mediums are sensitive to the disappointment of others in their work and react to disappointment individually. It is important to consider different perspectives and not assume all have the same agenda, experience or ethics.

Many years ago, I went to see a mediumship demonstration at a large venue in London. The medium was world renowned in his work and frequently mentioned in the media. I expected the demonstration to last an hour, but after ten minutes he sat down and said "the link isn't there anymore." He then pulled his chair to the edge of the stage and offered to host a question-and-answer session. This continued for another 30 minutes and was a very interesting session. I appreciated his honesty and in reality, he did his mediumship well - despite it being for a short length of time.

Some were disappointed as they had hoped to receive a spirit communication through his mediumship, but most appreciated his honesty and integrity. There is never a guarantee that someone will be the receiver of the public spirit communication and we need more focus on the reasonable expectations of mediums.

We need complete honesty about spirit intelligence and the human capacity to work with it.

8

FALSE FLAGS AND THE VAPOURS

We attribute some events to the phenomena of spirit intelligence, when they are not. Once it is realised that spirit are the innocent party it is usually funny and often a relief too.

There are many occasions when I have had to question whether a phenomenon, has been related to spirit intelligence. One that stands out in my memory, happened in my maisonette in Great Missenden. I lived upstairs and beneath me lived a young mother and her daughter. The location was a lovely place to live, with views over the hills and fields of rural Buckinghamshire. Being on the outer edge of the village, the neighbourhood was naturally peaceful.

Since my mid-twenties, I have practised transcendental meditation (TM). I had seen the positive results in a friend of mine and decided it would be a good idea to learn it, too. I took a course in Harrogate when I lived in North Yorkshire and discovered what it is like to transcend conscious thought and still be completely aware of everything around me. This I have found has been a great asset in my spiritual path - especially with trance mediumship and the importance of not influencing communication from my mind.

On a warm summer afternoon at home, I sat for TM for twenty minutes.

I trained my mind through the technique, to return to usual consciousness after twenty minutes, without a prompt. Once the twenty minutes of meditation had elapsed, I opened my eyes and saw a bluish mist floating in front of me. It was hovering approximately three feet above the floor.

It reminded me of the etheric blueprint I had experienced in Birmingham, and I watched the mist gently undulate in front of me. It was beautiful. I was at peace and mentally I thanked spirit for the experience. The difference this time was the mist didn't disappear back into my body, as had occurred in my previous experience.

I became physically more conscious after the meditation and noticed a powerful aroma. It was the smell of sausages cooking! What a strange experience - an etheric blueprint and the smell of sausages?

I got out of my chair, went to the kitchen window and saw that my downstairs neighbour was hosting a barbecue. I had left the bathroom window open, which was directly above her cooking area, and the smoke had wafted into my home as I meditated. I laughed as I looked back at the 'etheric' barbecue smoke in my living room!

Another false flag occurred recently at home. I had gone to bed and had turned the lights off. Drifting into the time just before sleep arrives, I heard three loud knocks from the area of my bed cabinet.

My first thought was that it was my mind. Some years ago I went through a period of being woken by the sounds of gunshot or an explosion. Other times, I would drift to sleep and see a large flash of light. It always happened as I was just about to enter a deep sleep state. It felt so real that I would often turn to my wife Jackie and ask her if she had experienced it, too. She never did, and I assumed she had been so deeply asleep she had missed it. After all, she reminded me curtly, that when I asked her, it was me waking her up and not an explosion!

The explosions and gunshot incidents happened over several months and were quite disturbing. One night when I was working at the Arthur Findlay College, I lay in bed reading an online newspaper. It helped me unwind from a long day of working with spirit. I read an article in the news describing my nocturnal disturbances and it had a name. It wasn't a long Latin phrase, or a disease named after the scientist who discovered it. It's called....Exploding Head Syndrome! Oh, goodness what a name and not one I'd seriously list on a medical form. Yet it described my experiences perfectly and was more common than I realised.

In brief, my symptoms were classic of this syndrome (that I can't take the name of seriously). The causes are hypothetical at this stage, but current thinking is an ear imbalance, stress or neurological activity. It appears to be benign. After a few months of experiencing exploding head syndrome, it stopped.

Fast Forward a few years to living in the West of Ireland and I was now experiencing large rapping noises in the bedroom, as I tried to sleep. This time, it was Jackie who also heard it and said, "what was that?" I told her I did not know and just as I did, it happened again.

Referencing the Hydesville rappings with the Fox sisters, Jackie asked if it was spirit communication. I couldn't sense a presence. It didn't show any awareness of us and it wasn't saying or doing anything appropriate to our situation. I concluded probably not and hoped it would stop.

It didn't stop and every few minutes, we heard three loud raps in the same place. The only thing left to do, so we had a chance of sleep was to turn the light on and discover the origin of the rappings.

As I sat on the edge of the bed, staring at my bedside cabinet, I found the culprit. It was my Apple Watch, and I physically watched it jump three times, face down on the surface of my cabinet. I removed the watch from the room, and the rest of the night was undisturbed.

The next day I searched the internet for the phenomena of the rapping Apple Watch. I discovered that when the battery is too low; it sends out three warning pulses. If you are wearing the watch, it feels like three gentle taps on the wrist. On a wooden bedside cabinet and face down, it sounds like loud rappings.

In the Dandenong mountains in Australia, is a conference centre called The Country Place. Each year the well loved mediums Tony Stockwell and

Lynn Probert, host a week long spiritual development retreat. In 2012, 2013 and 2015, I joined them
in the teaching team. Working in Australia is
incredible. The people took me to their hearts, and I
fell in love with Australia, its wildlife, scenery and
easygoing way of life. I would make several more
trips to Australia beyond the seminar work and
travelled throughout this incredible country,
teaching and making life-long friends.

On my second visit to the country place, a young
woman on the retreat asked to speak to me. She
told me she knew I had an interest in physical
mediumship and she would love to have a discussion about it. I agreed, but it was difficult to find
some free time. We kept passing in the corridor and
both acknowledging the promise with the words
"later."

Towards the end of the week, it preyed heavily on
my mind that we were running out of time to have
this conversation. The next time we passed, she
stopped and looked shocked. She said slowly with
emphasis on each word "I can actually see you are
physical medium yourself." I had to rush but again
said I would try to catch her later for our talk.

That evening, she passed me again in the corridor
and just said "there it is again - physical medi-

umship." I stopped and asked her what she could see and she told me I kept 'leaking ectoplasm' from my mouth!

It took me a few moments to realise what she could see and when I did; I laughed so much, I couldn't get my breath!

I had given up smoking, and the only way I stopped successfully was by vaping. Sometimes, after a taking a puff on my vape, the resulting mist would continue for a few minutes.

What she had witnessed were the residual wisps of water vapour still escaping from my mouth, after I had been vaping earlier! This was the ectoplasm in her mind! Once explained, we later had an evening drink and much laughter too.

Once you dedicate yourself to working with spirit intelligence, we frequently deem the unexplained spiritually culpable. Exploring the intelligence of a phenomenon through presence, emotional and social intelligence, helps us discern. Practical investigation may reveal another cause. Common sense should prevail before we blame the spirit world for every unexplained event. Metaphorically, I imagine the spirit world, shaking its head and tutting with rolled eyes, at many of the incidents we blame them for.

9

PORTENTS OF SPIRIT
INTELLIGENCE

A portent is a 'sign' that something significant is about to happen. Portents (also called omens) could be spirit intelligence preparing us for what is about to happen.

I wrote earlier about the father who saved his son's life by appearing in his car. As a sign of how the spirit makes its presence known intelligently, the continued protection of our loved ones is the noblest of causes. Unconditional love from beyond the grave is immortal.

When a loved one passes to spirit, many report unexpected signs, which may be attributed to the event. Previously, I wrote about the blue light around my son's hands when his grandfather passed. In my mother's experiences, spiders were her portents!

My mother was psychic and also encountered spirit intelligence from the afterlife. When her own father passed to spirit, she told me she knew he had gone, before confirmation arrived.

At eighty years of age, my grandfather passed away. Despite poor health for years, he was on holiday and enjoying life when he died. We might have expected his death had he been in hospital. But he had been actively enjoying life and well enough to take a brief holiday with his second wife and her family. After an evening meal and entertainment, he went to bed. The next morning he woke up and said he didn't feel too well. His wife asked the hotel to call the doctor. My grandfather closed this eyes and passed away in his bed, before the doctor arrived.

The evening before he died, my mother relaxed by watching the television, when I noticed her gaze was following something across the room. She looked troubled, so I asked if she was ok. 'Yes,' she replied, although I knew she was unsettled.

The morning of my grandfather's passing, she got herself ready for work and walked to the bus stop. As the bus approached, she noticed something wasn't right. The bus number should have been 17, but it stated it was 80 (same as my grandfather's age). As she stepped on the bus, she asked the driver if the number or the route had changed. He apologised and said he had forgotten to correct it before he left the depot. She took her seat and in fifteen minutes she stepped off and entered the building of her office.

As my mother opened the building door, she left it to close behind her. Unexpectedly, she felt someone pull the door back again. Realising she must have let the door almost slam shut on someone, she turned and apologised. Nobody was there.

As she climbed the staircase to her office, the phone was already ringing. It was my eldest sister who, as a solicitor, was an executor for my grandfather. She was calling to inform my mother of his passing. My mother picked up the phone and as soon as she heard my sister's voice say 'hello' she stated she knew her father had passed.

I came home from school and immediately knew something was wrong, as my mother was home before me. She told me the news and also that she knew he had gone, before she was officially told.

The evening before, when she had looked so troubled and distracted, she had seen spider on a leaf, float across the room. She had seen this clairvoyantly, but she explained that whenever she saw that, she knew someone was going to die soon. With many things seeming out of place the next morning, she just knew that when she answered my sister's call and heard her voice, it was her father who had died.

On November 16th 2020, I woke up and saw a small spider on the windowsill. I didn't mention it to Jackie as she doesn't like them. I decided to collect it and put it outside, but when I looked again it had gone!

It was also my birthday that day. Jackie wished me a happy birthday. I felt blessed to receive birthday cards, phone messages, emails and social media posts, congratulating me.

Before lunchtime I received a call from one of my sisters informing me that my mother had just passed unexpectedly at her nursing home.

On celebrating the day my mother brought me into the world, she physically had to take her leave. I was sad but grateful, as her passing was as perfect as it could be for her. She had enjoyed morning activities at the home and then felt tired. She then went back to her room for a rest and passed in her chair within a few minutes. She had no pain and was active until the last minutes of her life here. She had always said she hoped her passing was as easy as her father's and she got her wish. In the evening, I remembered the spider connection.

It may be difficult to analyse the intelligence of spirit in similar terms to ESi, when it applies to portents. In such cases as impending death, it would be difficult to cope with the power and presence of spirit if the person was still alive.

However, many do report that leading up to a passing, unusual things are said or done, that on reflection, often make more sense once the person has passed. My grandfather's wife remarked how he had become more sentimental and expressed much greater affection, in the days prior to his death, than he had ever done before.

Portents are also known on a psychic level, unrelated to physical death. Accounts of thinking about someone when they are unwell, when nobody had confirmed this, are commonplace. There are many accounts of being conscious of the presence of a person when they are physically far away and later discovering they were thinking of you at the same time. I often smell my grandfather's pipe tobacco, yet he passed over 45 years ago. The fields of intelligence have no boundaries of time or distance.

10

PERSONAL SIGNS OF SPIRIT INTELLIGENCE

Many people believe they experience 'signs' when their loved ones who have passed are close by. When we are feeling emotional, or need to make an important decision, a specific sight, sound or feeling of one of these signs brings great comfort or clarity to a situation. Signs may reassure us that our loved ones are still aware of our lives and wish to assist.

Some of the most common signs attributed to spirit intelligence are:

• White feathers

• Butterflies

• Dragonflies

• Birds

Other signs include specific songs being played on the radio and also scents that remind us of them. What makes them significant is that they usually appear when we least expect them. We do not engineer the timing of them for our own needs.

It is possible that we could influence what we believe are the 'signs from spirit' with our subconscious minds. Maybe an element of wishful thinking occurs sometimes. We may look for signs and be grasping at straws within grief. Part of the dilemma with personal signs is that we may explain it as the law of attraction. We desire something and subsequently notice more opportunities to manifest it, which consolidates a belief that the universe made it happen.

When we are not grieving, we are not trying to manifest any signs, so we don't notice symbolism around us as much. Yet many of the signs we read or hear of, which we relate to spirit, occur spontaneously, unexpectedly and are inexplicable.

Many of the commonly experienced 'signs of spirit' started their association through a random encounter. When the presence of a sign appears to be unusual and we are grieving, we might assign relevance as a heavenly sign. We may agree some signs between each other, before we pass. Should the bereaved party experience the sign, it is of great comfort to them. Some people agree a phrase or a code will be offered through a medium, if it is genuinely them communicating.

The broadcaster Gloria Hunniford, lost her tv presenter daughter Caron to breast cancer in 2004. Caron believed in angels and that a white feather was a 'calling card' from an angel or a spirit loved one and mentioned this many times to Gloria. She told her mother prior to her passing that she would let her know she was fine after she passed away.

At the funeral, from a clear sky dropped a large white feather. There was no bird to be seen, and the feather was witnessed by many. Since then, Gloria has recounted many occasions when she has received a white feather and it is a wonderful reminder to her that her daughter is close by with the angels. Whether you believe it, it has helped Gloria and has personal significance.

I had my experience with white feathers recently. I was taken into hospital with a lung exacerbation at the height of the COVID-19 outbreak. I was on a covid assessment ward for a few hours until they returned my test as negative. They subsequently took me to medical ward.

I had a disturbed night on a noisy ward and only fell asleep briefly in the early hours of the morning. However, when I awoke, there were three large pure white feathers on my bed. In my mind I said thank you and still do not know how they came to be there. Perhaps someone put them there? Perhaps I hallucinated them? Perhaps an angel was looking after me? It didn't matter, because it brought some comfort that I was being cared for.

Many signs have a symbolic meaning. A Native American belief is that the feather symbolises higher wisdom and importance. We associate the white colour with the pure light realms of spirit and also the crown chakra. Others believe they are from angels' wings for healing and protection.

Butterflies often become signs of spirit intelligence when they appear in usual places. Especially soon after the passing of loved one. Examples include, in winter, inside the room where someone passed and even resting on a person, despite them attempting to brush it aside. The butterfly symbolises meta-morphosis, beauty, ascension, strength through fragility.

The dragonfly symbolises similar qualities to the butterfly and represents the added quality of adap-tation. It moves swiftly and changes direction quickly. We usually find it near a source of water and water is symbolically the carrier of emotions. The dragonfly also symbolises an emerging new state of being. Its iridescent wings reveal beauty with abundant light.

The question will always arise that signs are merely the bereaved looking for hope. We are looking for them and adopting them as our personal signs from those we love, as a way of keeping their love close. The hope within the sign validates the belief that they haven't gone from us forever. This may be true in many cases, but others have experiences that would defy this explanation.

With the Amazon Alexa incident and my brother's playlist of songs, I didn't want any signs or any mediums offering to make a connection. I was too angry and just wanted him here in this world again. My family felt we had been robbed, as the GP had ignored all the red flags of his cancer, in the early curable stages. I didn't want a sign from heaven. I wanted him back at home with his wife, seeing his children and grandchildren again.

Music is something that brings us together and has a lot of emotion and memories invested within. If my brother had any influence on what happened, it made sense to me that he would do it through the universal medium of music. I believe this made it bearable.

Signs of spirit intelligence don't have to originate from the afterlife and sometimes it is impossible to prove their origin. Some signs may originate from the spirit intelligence within us all - from the soul, or our intuition. Inexplicable signs don't need an origin - just gratitude, as I discovered in my studio one day.

I was sitting at my desk, catching up with paperwork in the studio. The studio was a large room with industrial strip lighting throughout. I realised a buzzing sound near my ear and waved my arm to get rid of whatever insect it was. As I looked up, I saw directly opposite me a large fly. I was relieved it was an insect without a sting.

The fly left the window and crashed into my forehead before flying back again to the window. I looked at it and swore. I communicate with animals but I was not in the mood to start a dialogue with this aggressive fly! I continued my work, but the fly kept diving at me! It was becoming personal now. The attacks intensified, and I was being constantly bombarded by it.

In frustration, I rose from my chair and stepped back. As I did this, the entire lighting unit above my desk came crashing down. Had I not moved, it would have hit me on the head. I never saw the fly again but in my mind I said 'thank you.'

Signs of spirit intelligence of psychic origin may be linked to intuition and have saved many lives. Everyone has a tale to tell about when they had a gut feeling and with good cause. In my Father's case, it involved his time in the RAF as a pilot and post-war active duty.

On the rare occasions my father engaged in conversation, he was most animated when it involved his service life. During the Second World War he was an RAF pilot and for two years after the war ended, they stationed him in the Far East. He worked repatriating prisoners of war and other post-war duties.

The high point of being in the far east, were the flights to Hong Kong. All the pilots wanted this route, as during the stopover, they visited the bustling markets and enjoyed the nightlife. Before the servicemen went home on leave, they always tried to get a trip to Hong Kong, so they could browse the markets and buy presents for their families.

It was my father's turn to fly to Hong Kong, and he had been looking forward to it for a long time. On the morning of his flight, another pilot asked if he would give up his seat as he was about to go on leave soon and wanted to go to the markets. My father understood but was unhappy. He had waited for his turn patiently. As he was considering the request, he described to me he felt a strange sense of anxiety whenever he thought about the trip to Hong Kong. Believing this to be simply his own disappointment, he dismissed the feeling. He reluctantly gave up his seat as a gesture of goodwill.

That flight and all the crew were lost in the ocean and never recovered. The strange sense of anxiety served to save his life some years later, too.

In the late 1950's, my father was stationed in Cyprus during the island conflict between Turkey and Greece. His unit was sent to inspect an abandoned property, suspected to be a hideout. As his unit approached, they were instructed to enter the building from the front. My father experienced the same sense of anxiety he felt about the Hong Kong flight. He signalled he was going to approach from the back of the property. This was directly against orders, but he insisted, knowing he would be reprimanded later. As he went around the back he heard a massive explosion. He was bleeding badly from a shrapnel wound, but sadly most of his unit had succumbed to the booby trapped front door. My father survived with just a scar. The others on that fateful day never made it home again.

Birds are powerful symbols and many have mythical qualities, such as the Phoenix and the Native American Thunderbird. Symbolically the bird is a messenger, able to change locations, communicate sound and share its song with the world. There are many deathbed stories about birds appearing either in the room or at a window when someone is passing to spirit. One particular bird often associated as a visitation from the spirit world is the robin. Robins are territorial, so we do see them alone and in the same locations. If we notice one soon after the passing of a loved one, it is common to associate it with them.

I enjoyed many 'over the fence' conversations with my neighbour John, when I lived in Chesham, Buckinghamshire. We shared a love of being outside and gardening. Every conversation was precious, as John was terminally ill with colon cancer. Over the months he lost weight and got weaker, but we still chatted regularly.

On one occasion, a robin landed on the fence between us and stayed for the duration of our conversation. From that day onwards, the same robin joined us every time we met. It always positioned itself between us and stayed for as long as we did. It fascinated us how trusting the robin was, as it was very close to us and didn't fly off if we laughed or shifted our feet.

One day, John mentioned his daughter worked at IBM in Portsmouth. My brother had worked there too until his recent early retirement. The next time I saw John he brought a photo with him of his daughter at a company dinner. Next to her was sat my brother! It felt like the world had become smaller. John checked with his daughter and I with my brother and they both remembered each other well. To live so far away from our relatives and discover the next-door neighbour is connected in some way to your family is a rare synchronicity.

A few months later, John passed away from the cancer. The robin was still waiting on the fence where we used to talk. I started to say "hi John" each time I spotted it. Every robin was John in my mind now, and I acknowledge each one the same way.

15 years later, my brother passed away from the same cancer. It was and still is devastating for our family. It was unclear if I would be well enough to attend his funeral. Luckily I made it, as you will have read from the incident with the amazon echo

dot. During the interim, I asked his wife about his favourite flowers, so I could plant them here in his memory. He loved azaleas, so Jackie and I purchased an azalea bush and she planted it in the garden. Every time I go outside and look at it, there is robin on the branch of the tree near it. Now I say hello to John and my brother. I know it's not them, but it is a reminder to stop and remember them both for a few moments. We never forget our friends and loved ones, but sometimes a 'sign' stops us from ignoring an important moment. This year the azalea is vibrant with pink flowers and the robin is always there to sing.

We can call it intuition, a gut feeling, precognition, wishful thinking, synchronicity etc. we can also call it spirit intelligence as we are spirit too and some-where within the spirit, this intelligence is a sign that calls to us. Sometimes it will save our lives, sometimes a song, a feather, a creature or a scent will bring us closer to our loved ones for a moment. The signs of spirit intelligence are real to us - what-ever the origin. More than anything - the signs have the power to reconnect us back to the love.

11

EVIDENCE UNKNOWN

"Please, can you just fit in one extra sitting? This one is urgent, and I know you are exhausted, but they are friends of mine and really need your help," my host pleaded.

Indeed, I was exhausted, but us medium's find it difficult to say no, when someone is desperate for hope. I already had a list of appointments to work through that evening but my host expressed an urgency that I fit in a particular married couple during my break.

I didn't know their names when they entered the small sitting room to meet me. A middle - aged couple who looked as if the weight of the world was upon them. The husband was sobbing gently, his wife looked shocked.

I greeted them, invited them to sit and offered water and tissues. It all seemed so inadequate compared to their mental state of what I can only describe as 'broken.'

I was teaching a weekend workshop of mediumship and working with healing colours in Ireland and part of the deal was to offer a few sittings. Inevitably, as the weekend progressed, participants reported back to their friends and families and the list for sittings grew beyond what I expected.

We sat, and I explained how I worked and how I only wanted them to let me know if they could or couldn't validate my findings. I promised I would do my best for them.

As I took a deep breath and invited the spirit world to join us, an image of a young man on a racing bicycle flashed through my mind. He was around 20 years of age, dressed in professional cycling clothes, and had a gigantic smile on his face. I relayed this first impression, and the couple looked at each other, then turned back to me and said please continue - it's him!

From that moment, the information flowed. He was indeed a keen road racing cyclist, young, a fitness fanatic, and thrilled to see his parents again. "It's Joe," I said to the couple, and they nodded.

As the sitting progressed, Joe showed me his life of fitness, his love of music, his new apartment, and much more. He also showed me how his dad was keeping his bike polished, oiled, and in pristine condition.

Significantly he showed me in great detail an image of his sudden passing. What I saw clairvoyantly was an image of a human heart with the artery detaching between the heart and kidney. He was at the gym when it happened and it was so fast; he didn't make it to the hospital before passing.

Reassuring his parents, he shared with me he didn't suffer and he was now with his beloved Granda Tom. He spoke of many happy memories and offered gratitude for an amazing life with them. His parents were laughing and smiling at the quirky family jokes he shared through me, as evidence it was genuinely him. The room filled with a lightness.

We shared much information, and the tears flowed again - but this time for joy. As our time was ending, I asked him for a lasting message. His words were "tell them I enjoyed playing the guitar, and I was quite good." At this, both his parents looked at me and his father said that he didn't play guitar or even own one!

It confused me. Everything had been so clear, specific and spot on! I tried to find out more, but he just repeated the same information. I felt flat and had to admit that perhaps I was getting too tired and got it wrong. It was a sad moment to leave the sitting on that last message, but you have to be true to spirit. You can't adapt or change the genuine message from spirit.

I continued with another couple of sittings that went smoothly. My last of the evening was a young lady and as she entered, Joe on his racing bike came hurtling back through the images in my mind. "That's my girl" said Joe. she confirmed she was Joe's girlfriend and as the sitting progressed, Joe revealed she was still living in the apartment they had just rented together, before he passed. He also mentioned other moments, such as how yesterday she put a rose quartz, crystal angel on his grave.

Again, everything went well, and Joe was a great communicator. As she arose to leave, I asked her if she knew about him playing a guitar? She burst out laughing and said yes! Not long before Joe passed, he bought a secondhand guitar and was trying to learn to play it. The reason his parents didn't know about it was that he wanted to surprise them by playing the guitar at their upcoming silver wedding celebration.

The intelligence of Joe's communication was evidenced to his parents & girlfriend when he communicated the awareness of their everyday lives. He did this via the connection to his bike and the rose quartz angel - amongst several other pieces of information.

He knew the right thing to say to his parents, which at the time was to give information about a guitar; of which they had no prior knowledge. He also expressed his awareness of his current situation by mentioning his Granda and saying his name.

They received the guitar validation soon after their sitting was over. Joe's girlfriend phoned them immediately, and it was a special moment in their shared grief, where they supported their loving bond for Joe.

Joe will have known that his girlfriend was booked for a sitting and found an intelligent way to show factual knowledge both known, unknown and revealed later.

You can never be the same again after losing someone so young and so suddenly. The grief is unimaginable unless you have experienced it. But Joe's parents reported back that to know that Joe had acknowledged their anniversary in such an amazing way, brought great comfort and reassurance.

Thank you Joe.

12

THE FORGOTTEN EVIDENCE

For mental mediumship, the unidentified evidence is both the bane and the blessing of the medium. On the one hand, you have the intelligence of the spirit confirming the sanctity and intelligence of their communication, versus the frustration of not being understood at the very moment of what you hoped would be a positive validation.

In public mediumship, that moment can appear critical. Standing on a platform with a denial of what you, as the medium is relaying, is confidence busting for all. You feel confused, disappointed and exposed. It's like a dream where only you are naked and you feel incredibly vulnerable.

In that moment, you try to make sense of the information, explain it another way, go back to spirit for clarification, take a moment and try again and sometimes you just have to leave it and move forward to the next communication. The toughest scenario is when it is your last spirit communication of the event, as you have ended the demonstration on what feels like a low point. It can feel very disappointing.

This happens to all mediums in public and it leads to some sleepless nights and soul searching.

Many years ago, I was the last mediumship demonstration of the public service at the Arthur Findlay College. I had time for three communications and the first two went well. The third and final contact was going very well until I was given some specific evidence from a father in spirit to his daughter about her responsibility for looking after the money and payments for household bills. It was so specific and extraordinary that I even clairvoyantly saw her as a very young child with large quantities of cash being wrapped in brown paper and putting it inside her school satchel - to be paid on her way home from school! It appeared to be an extraordinary responsibility for a young school-child, but it was revealed to me. Yet it was met with a "no" and I was stuck. I couldn't do anything else but move on with the message rather blandly and then finish.

The energy of the room fell flat! I saw my colleagues' eyes darting between themselves, exchanging concerned expressions.

Yet the next day the person in question asked to see me privately and explained it was all true. She had simply forgotten. She was so upset about this and I reassured her it was fine. Secretly, my pride took a small beating, but I was happy her father had been right and, ultimately, I had delivered the correct information.

For me this was fine, but it's a harsh experience when it occurs and we must as mediums emphasise that denying information is something we all must keep an open mind about. Time will eventually deliver the final verdict, yet we can't claim the recipient is wrong as that would humiliate them.

Naturally, the medium's disappointment at getting a blank response to information is not the concern of the spirit. We can go from high to low in seconds and it is a tough experience to make sense of and often disturbs the medium's thoughts for hours - sometimes days afterwards.

This can also happen in the private sitting too and although you may have more scope to explore the information and work out what it means, it can still lead to disappointment.

What if your recipient has a poor memory and forgets a significant aspect of evidence? What if it was so long ago and in the moment of receiving information via a medium, they just can't recall such information? What if their expectations of you cloud their recall?

This also happened some years ago when I lived in a small maisonette in Buckinghamshire. I was busy conducting one-to-one sittings at home. I had a policy that if I or the sitter weren't happy with the quality of the sitting, there was no charge. In fact, I was pretty tough on myself and many times refused payment because of my sense of the sitting not having been as good, as I considered it should have been.

There are drawbacks to this approach and first, it can be that you have set the bar too high and are doing yourself a disservice. Most professional mediums are extremely tough on themselves, despite often doing their job well, will still believe they could have done more. It's a sign of a serious medium who finishes a sitting, or a platform demonstration and spends some time reviewing what they could have done better!

Second, when you become caught up in whether you were good enough, you may have ignored that your time and experience are precious and deserve respect too.

We may often hear the expression that when someone books a sitting, they are paying for your time. That is true but they have also expected a service and a service which you may have promised, should deliver results by achieving objectives. If it's time alone with you - then you don't need to be a medium to do this. You could merely advertise yourself as someone to spend time with!

If you have given your time and also delivered what you said you would, then a refund is unnecessary. The genuine issue is fear. Too many mediums have heard or experienced the criticism that we are making money from the grief or misery of others and are sensitive to this belief. It is this criticism which fuels us to be perfectionists and to be accepted. Also, many sitters are concerned about their own gullibility because of sceptical perceptions of mediums.

Yet a job done, time invested, ethically delivered and objectives achieved, are worthy challengers to us all.

13

___

GRUMMY AND BADGER

On one particular afternoon, two young women had booked a sitting and arrived on time. I opened the door and was immediately struck by how young they both appeared. One looked to be in her late teens and the other - early twenties. Both were very emotional, and I fetched some hot tea, tissues for their tears and we had a few minutes of general chat, so they could settle their emotions.

It is quite common for a sitter to become over-whelmed from the first moment of contact with a medium. There is often so much hope 'pinned' on the sitting that when it becomes reality, the emotion is overwhelming. I felt maternal towards them as they both looked so bereft; that had I known them as friends, my instinct would have been to offer a hug.

They didn't look similar, so I made the assumption they were unrelated and that one was an accompanying friend for support, or that they were two friends who both wanted a sitting. Yet only one sitting was booked with me. I clarified this, and it transpired they were sisters who had the same interest in whoever could communicate from spirit.

As I began, I became aware clairvoyantly of two women in spirit. One was young and the other elderly, yet they were clearly together as I sensed the bond of love between them. I relayed this information, and both nodded and smiled.

I prefer not to have more than one spirit communicator and usually, simply asking for the most significant one at this moment, to come to the fore works well. As I asked for this, the younger lady moved back in my mind's eye and the elderly woman remained foremost. Clairaudiently, I heard a gentle voice state "I'm Grummy!"

My first thought was that my mind was playing tricks on me and really I should hear Granny. I explained that I thought I had Granny with me, and they both nodded in agreement. However, it just didn't feel quite right and as I asked the spirit with me for clarification, I heard in my mind "not Granny - Grummy!"

I had to share this, but hesitated at first. One of the most difficult aspects of honing your mediumship is trusting your information. In moments of distrust, the medium could resort to accepting a 'yes' as sufficient, or becoming general and non-specific in the information they offer. The difficulty this presents is that the sitting becomes too generic and we miss the truly unique intelligence from spirit.

With a questioning tone I said "does Grummy mean anything to you?" - with that the two young women laughed, shrieked and also shed a few happy tears. When they had regained composure, they explained that the younger lady I had seen was their mother who had passed to spirit shortly after the birth of the youngest sister. Their Granny had parented both of them. As result, Granny had two roles, and they renamed her Grummy from their childhood and they always called her by this name. Grummy knew exactly what she wanted me to say - her social intelligence knew that her special name would confirm her reassuring presence without a doubt, to her two granddaughters.

The rest of the sitting went very well with Grummy bringing beautiful memories of their lives and much evidence that she was still enjoying a 'sing along' with her husband and daughter, also in spirit.

Their mother also came forward again and made communication with her daughters. But Grummy's life and passing was closer to them now and I could sense their interest was less than enthusiastic for the mother, who had sadly been absent for most of their years. Without prompting, the elder sister told me they had no memories anymore of their mother and what life with her was like. Grummy had done her best to keep her memory alive, but the sisters thought of Grummy as the mother figure in their lives and it was she they had hoped to hear from.

Undeterred, their mother clairvoyantly showed me three things. First was a wedding ring, second an image of her eldest daughter, and third was an old black and white wedding photo.

The eldest sister confirmed she was engaged to be married but couldn't understand about the old wedding photo. I asked for a moment to get more information and the mother brought my attention to a small lady in the front row of the wedding party, with dark hair and a white streak of hair across the top of her head. I clairaudiently heard her say the name Aunty Badger! As I repeated this to the sisters, they looked quite blank and said they didn't know who she was or the name. It deflated me.

I had found Grummy, but their mother who had worked hard to be there was not being understood, or I had a wild imagination. It was time to stop.

I berated myself for a poor sitting and refused to charge them my fee. For days it bothered me how clear the information was and how unique Aunty Badger appeared. She was so distinctive that if a stranger saw her, they would remember - yet the sisters did not recognise her.

It was over a year later that I heard from the sisters again. They had emailed me and specifically requested a sitting for Mother's Day that year. I didn't need to be Sherlock Holmes to realise that they wanted to hear from their mother - but which one? The one who raised them (Grummy)? or the one who gave birth to them?

They arrived promptly at 2pm on Mother's day and with big smiles, handed me a beautiful bunch of daffodils. We sat down and I began.

This time their mother was to the fore of my clairvoyance and Grummy in the background. I questioned whether the significance of the day was influencing my mind, but thought better of it and told myself to trust again.

The sisters were delighted and said they needed to thank her and tell her they are fine and doing well. It was then that the emotional intelligence of the previous sitting became clear.

"We have a confession," said the eldest sister. "We know who Aunty Badger is, and she was exactly as you described." The youngest reached into her handbag and produced an old black and white photo of a wedding party and there she was - exactly as their mum had shown me before!

I was astounded, but grateful, and joked about how they should pay me double now. Yet the evidence was so clever and I was amazed by what unfolded since our first meeting with what was about to transpire.

After the first sitting, the sisters reflected upon it. Their minds were so fixated on hearing from Grummy that everyone else was blocked out of their memory, or not given consideration.

When subsequently, one of them remembered Aunty Badger, they set about going through the boxes from Grummy's attic (which was full of old photo albums) hoping to locate this photo I described. They eventually found it, but they also found so much more. As they reminisced over the family photos, two letters fell from between the pages of the album. There was one for each sister, written by their mother when she was dying of cancer. In each letter she wished them a wonderful life, told them how proud she was of them and that she would always love them. She also wrote that she would find a way to let them know she was still close to them.

In the communication on mother's day, it became clear that she knew that they had only wanted to hear from Grummy. When I first met the sisters, their mother also knew that Grummy had lost the letters she needed them to receive. By showing the wedding photo and focussing on a forgotten aunt, her emotional intelligence knew that in the future, they would investigate. In the investigation of the photo, they would find the most important letters she ever had to write for her girls!

Both sisters told me they felt reassured their loved ones really were looking out for them and it had brought them both a beautiful peace, they hadn't known of before.

Thank you to the wonderful Mum, Grummy & Aunty Badger in spirit.

14

PSYCHIC SPIRIT INTELLIGENCE

Psychic spirit intelligence is exciting! Most will relate to 'gut feelings' and we rely on them in all walks of life. From doctors having a sense there is something else beyond the medical results in front of them, to the detective having a hunch about a suspect. Science and physical evidence may not give us all the answers but are essential. The hunch is like a signpost. Together they build a significant story. Psychic spirit intelligence is therefore part of our lives and is the invisible, hidden store of knowledge, that offers directions, perspectives and validations.

Around 2005 - 2007, I was regularly visited by the county coroner. I would be handed a pile of sealed files and asked to say what impressions I received. Not knowing any names or details was very liberating as I could focus purely on my intuition. There were files where I sensed so much information and others where I felt nothing at all. One time, I came to learn that the files where I had felt nothing were actually empty apart from blank paper. In experimental terms, I imagined this was akin to the control required in research.

As each file was passed to me, I would sit with it, close my eyes and place a hand on the front and the back, so it was sandwiched between them. Sometimes, I sensed heat, or I saw an image of something, or a smell, or numbers. I trusted the process to be what it was without any expectation.

For a long time I didn't question the coroner - I just held the files and mentioned how I felt and what I saw and experienced.

After several visits, we had our final meeting, as I would be soon moving to live in another area. I asked what was the purpose of me doing this, as he needed physical evidence, backed by science in his cases. He agreed that anything I said couldn't be used as part of his investigations. However, before he made a ruling on a case, he wanted to be sure he hadn't missed an area of investigation. My findings could help him look at a case with a fresh perspective, even though it wouldn't feature in an inquest.

As it was our last meeting I asked him if anything had helped. He assured me that as a result of the information I had offered, a case that was going to be ruled upon as suicide, had resulted in him asking for more information and was now a major murder investigation! I was glad to help in any way I could.

Psychic spirit intelligence is the intuition that is the language of the soul. Through an awareness of emotional energy, intention and attunement, a good psychic reader discovers information and is able to offer helpful insights.

The spirit intelligence from those who have passed over, is not always necessary, or desired. As a medium myself, I have no need to know that my loved ones are ok and communicate with them. I know it already! Instead, if I needed some spirit intelligence, I'd be more likely to seek a good psychic who can use their intuition to help. I would seek out their ability if I couldn't work out for myself a dilemma, or just needed some validation of something in my life.

Psychic intelligence is often associated with:

• General psychic readings

• Tarot or oracle card readings

The skilled psychic, attunes to the subject and in the context of intent, reveals the influences. As an example, If I were to consult a psychic, I would expect to be asked what I was seeking answers about. If I were to ask for insight about my career, the psychic will attempt to uncover my strengths and weaknesses, hopes and desires, successes and failures, the past, present and likely direction of my career. They will also, discover the obstacles and identify the triumphs. This is just a small sample of possibilities, yet the key issue is that it is not about knowing our loved ones in spirit still live - it's about us and making sense of life. It empowers us with self - knowledge that we are often too close to, to see objectively.

The spirit intelligence of the psychic is not only discovered by 'reading' the energy of the sitter and intuitively analysing it. It works with inanimate object too. We see this in a practice known as psychometry.

Psychometry involves reading energetic impressions or memories that have been stored. The fabric of buildings store energy , which is why a good psychic can discover much about the history of a place, without advance knowledge.

15

NELSON MANDELA LOVED
INSTANT COFFEE

From what appeared to be a regular evidential mediumship sitting, I soon entered a period of work which included many celebrities, royalty and the aristocracy. I had given a sitting to a lady who was seeking evidence of her mother in spirit. The sitting went well, but unbeknownst to me, she was a well regarded therapist with an elite clientele.

A week after her sitting, she asked if I could come to her house in Berkshire and conduct a day of sittings. She would arrange lunch and cover my expenses, plus her clients would pay me directly.

I arrived at her house and was stopped at the gate by special branch officers. I glimpsed they were wearing guns beneath their jackets and one held the leash of a well behaved German Shepard dog. They asked for my driving license and then

92

directed me where to park. I was unnerved as I had no idea why they were there.

Before I could turn around and drive away (I wanted to at this point) my host opened the door, flung her arms around me and with the biggest smile invited me in. "I don't want you to feel intimidated, so I didn't tell you who would be here." That suited me perfectly as the least I knew, the happier I would be, knowing I didn't have time to form any subconscious ideas. I did make one request and that was there would be no guns in the room. She assured me the room had been security swept and nobody would have a gun in the room. Phew! I felt as if I had entered an alternate reality and was about to venture into the unknown. "Just do what you do and it will be fine" said my host.

She directed me to room and as I entered, I was eye to eye with a senior member of the British Royal family. At which point, I burst into laughter and retreated from the room. I could hear my sitter laughing too thankfully, as I couldn't contain my raucous belly laughs.

I had to compose myself and when I had, I walked back in, said hello, apologised and worked as I normally work. It all went very well and we ended up having a great discussion about spirituality.

The rest of the day was spent in sittings with more royalty and aristocracy. One lady in particular was delighted as she had herself trained as a medium and a healer covertly at the College of Psychic Studies and knew what was evidential and what was not. She liked how I worked and invited me to her house to give sittings to her family.

As I entered her estate, she had asked me in advance to stop at the gate and call her before driving to the front door. I did as requested and discovered the reason was so she could turn the huge, ornate fountain in front of the house on, before I arrived. It was an impressive stately home and before we had the sitting, she treated me to a tour of the gardens and her sculpture park. The sittings went well and she paid me generously, plus gave me a gift of sterling silver charms to keep in my purse. I still have them today.

Before I left, we had some tea and she asked me about a chair I was sat on. "Can you pick anything up from it?" She asked. I sat for a moment, quietened my mind and felt a presence around me. Simultaneously, I saw a smiling Nelson Mandela in my mind. She confirmed he had visited and sat in that same chair. Oh my I thought, I've sat in Nelson's chair! Our backsides had shared the same space! It felt unreal, but I was pushed for more information.

As I sat back again and focussed on the task, I had a vision of Nelson Mandela, drinking his coffee, whilst the house staff were running around looking very stressed, plus a jar of Nescafe instant coffee! It all seemed bizarre and disjointed, but turned out to make sense in the end.

My host had received a call one morning that her neighbour (another aristocrat) had Nelson Mandela staying with them during his UK visit. He mentioned that Mandela would like to meet her and could they come over for coffee now? Without hesitation my host said yes of course. Then realised they only had instant coffee in the house as the Fortnum and Mason's delivery hadn't arrived yet! She was in a panic that she could only give Nelson Mandela instant coffee. She was horrified he wouldn't have the finest coffee beans, freshly ground and brewed. She hurriedly sent a member of staff to buy some fresh coffee beans.

It was too late to wait for the coffee beans as Nelson Mandela was already walking up the long lawn to her house, with his friend. Nelson Mandela would have to drink Nescafe and so he did.

Whether it was politeness or absolute truth, Mandela said it was the best coffee he had ever drunk in Europe! The instant coffee was served in a silver pot with a side of fresh cream, brown sugar crystals in a bowl, with an antique silver spoon. All my host could focus upon was that is was instant coffee. I'm sure Nescafe would have been very proud to know the President of South Africa and a hero to so many, drank their product and hailed it the best in Europe.

I marvelled that by parking my backside in the same spot as Nelson, I came to learn all this and it still makes me laugh today!

Through intuition, I felt the energetic presence, saw clairvoyantly and the memories held the intelligence of awareness and recalling the appropriate things that were said.

16

THE FLOW STATE OF SPIRIT INTELLIGENCE.

The ability to receive the intelligence of spirit is certainly possible through mediumship, as my experiences have already shown me. Mediumship is when we engage ourselves as the 'broker' of spirit intelligence and then communicate it effectively. We discover the primary experiences of mediumship through:

• Clairvoyance (seeing images)

• Clairaudience (hearing sounds or words)

• Clairsentience (sensing information)

• Claircognisance (a sense of 'knowing' something)

Other awarenesses may be experienced as:

• Tastes

• Scents

• Physical sensations (such as tingling or a gentle tapping on the head)

Many mediums at some point will notice working with all available 'Clair' experiences. Yet, many describe themselves as dominant in only one area. It is commonplace to hear a medium describe themselves as using one ability - such as a clairaudience, or clairvoyance, clairsentience, etc.

Clairsentience is the 'catchall' method of receiving information through spirit intelligence. In all cases, we sense the information. Our mind senses an image, senses a sound, or an emotion - everything is sensed and interpreted by the mind. The manifestation of the intelligence in the mind is merely descriptive. I saw, I heard, I felt - is a mental interpretation. We may believe we are clairvoyant because we see images, but it involves all our senses to provide this information.

During my teaching career, I would often refer to the analogy of an iceberg when relating mediumship and spirit intelligence. In all encounters, we reveal only a small proportion of our lives and experiences. We can pick and choose.

If we go for a job interview, for example, we reveal what we want to reveal on or above the surface of our life experience. We choose the relevance we wish to project. We decide what information leaves an impression. We also leave out information about ourselves beneath the surface.

With spirit communication, we can use the same analogy. If we think of the iceberg above the water, here we find what the spirit needs us to know. We may even have to dip below the surface of the water. Mindful that the iceberg is dynamic, and the surface is in constant change is important. True spirit intelligence will show that the message is unique in each encounter.

The monumental challenge for many developing mediums is that they can confuse seeking spirit communication on human terms. This is impossible and will lead to disappointment. An expectation that a flowing verbal conversation with someone who is now deceased is possible is unrealistic. Once we remind ourselves that our loved ones in the spirit world are discarnate, we know they don't have an expressive physical voice, or body anymore. What we see, feel, or hear in the mind is a reconstruction of our senses. There are some brilliant shortcuts to spiritually intelligent communication, via the mind of the medium, being inspired by the spirit.

The intelligence from spirit often involves symbology or colour, which poses a challenge when we think communication is primarily words and moving pictures. I have often heard developing mediums say that they don't understand colour or symbology. Yet, the spirit is astute and suggests rather than insists. It offers an interpretation that either makes some sense to the medium, who can convey its meaning, or is understood by the intended recipient if it is offered without embellishment.

Learning more about colour and symbolism is certainly helpful. The information we store in the mind is a repository for spirit intelligence to express themselves. Colours and symbols are also expressions of emotion, health and energy and worthwhile tools to explore. Working with psychic skills such as tarot and oracle cards, pendulums, psychometry, all add to the library of intelligence that can be accessed in the mind.

The danger posed for credible mediums is from those who believe the spirit intelligence was given to them, when it actually originated from their own assumptions. It is then relayed and described as originating from spirit. This is quite easy to spot as it is usually generalised information, inappropriate, or too fanciful.

In my experience, the most significant mediumship with spirit intelligence occurs when there is no expectation and I am in a 'flow state.' Occasionally, I have experienced a snippet of what appears to be a video replay in the mind, but this is rare. On most occasions, a glimpse of an image or symbol has been the key to the spirit intelligence. Sometimes it is so fast, it is easily missed. A flow state allows for rapid information that achieves full attention to what arises.

Flow states are when you are totally focussed, immersed and engaged with what you are doing. A sense of time disappears and the creative mind is at its most engaged. Many artists achieve flow states. They become so focussed on their craft that hours can pass, yet it feels like minutes. When you are deeply focused on an activity, your brain can enter a state of heightened focus.

Meditators, writers, healers, yoga students, musicians, athletes, frequently experience flow states. During the flow state, the creativity and inner strength are abundant. Outstanding works of art, states of calm, compositions of words and sounds reach a heightened level. A runner will pass through a pain barrier, then seemingly without effort, finish a marathon.

With flow states, the mind is free from physical distractions and mental chatter. The brain is flooded with 'feel good' endorphins and in this state, spirit intelligence is unhindered by the medium. With the focus on what arises from spirit and not the medium's mind, the senses awaken. The potential for spirit to paint images in our minds, a snippet of relevant sound, emotions, tastes and smells all becomes reality - becomes intelligent information.

This explains why respecting and understanding the influential power of our minds is vital to good mediumship. Working with the flow state takes us beyond being a generalist. We need serious focus to experience and present spirit intelligence. We need discipline to make it work.

17

NURTURING THE FLOW STATES

The key ingredients for nurturing the flow states for the intelligence of spirit to work are:

• Knowing your own spirit power

• Regular meditation

• The power of intention

Knowing your own spirit power is vital. You are a unique soul expressing the divine nature of yourself. This is easy to forget as we stumble through life, doing what we believe others expect of us. When you understand you have spirit power, there is a universal recognition of the uniqueness of others, too. There is a recognition that spirit is a life force expressed freely and in all our uniquenesses, relates to everything.

If you have been developing your mediumship, you may have been encouraged to use an exercise called 'Sitting In The Power.' It is specific to learning your own spirit power, the power of the life force, and our eternal relationship. A guided recording of sitting in the power can be found on my website or YouTube channel. Once you are accustomed, you may wish to sit without guidance. Either way, there is an opportunity to sit in the power, and it is for your spiritual growth.

Meditation has significantly assisted my mediumship path and given spirit intelligence a chance to express itself. The physical and mental health benefits of meditation are well documented and researched. From the perspective of mediumship, it is the ideal way to quieten the mental chatter of the mind and encourage focus.

I have meditated for over 30 years with transcendental meditation. I use a mantra at first and then after a short time; I enter a space of no thought, yet full awareness. As I end the meditation and my mind begins to activate with thoughts, and the most creative and inspirational moments arise.

There are many forms of meditation which result in quietening the mental traffic and improving focus.

Some work by focusing on the breath, or by chanting. A most popular form of meditation today is mindfulness.

Mindfulness is ideal for understanding your own thoughts and how you are affected by them. It creates a sense of observation and can help significantly with general mental health and problem solving. Meditation is personal and a means to quieten the mind - it is specific to you.

The power of intention is a key factor in mediumship and life in general. We associate intention as a something we plan to do. To use it effectively, intention is about being part of the doing. By this I mean we don't just want, we have to feel we are part of the outcome - experiencing it on a mental level first.

Experiments where athletes intentionally run their race in their minds, show that areas of the brain associated with specific muscles they would use, become highly active - just through intentional thought.

In mediumship, if we apply intention we can change our energy. If I am about to demonstrate mediumship on a stage, I spend some time visualising it flowing well, I'm feeling good, I'm in the zone. I recreate the feeling of it going well and how that feels. This really does help and also gives us focus for the task ahead.

18

FINDING FOCUS FROM A HOLLYWOOD ICON

The afternoon was busy with three sittings booked in. In the morning I sat in the power. After lunch I meditated to clear my mind and before the first sitting, I spent some moments of intention, imagining welcoming them and them looking happy as they left.

The afternoon went well and my last sitter arrived. He was mid-twenties and looked extremely sad. As I sat with him, I asked if he knew what a mediumship sitting was about. It shocked me when I heard I was the 10th that month he had seen.

This led to a conversation about whether he was seeking something that a medium couldn't offer. "No. I just haven't found the right one yet." Instantly, I felt a pressure but my senses got the better of me and I told myself I could only do what I can do!

As I connected to his friend in spirit who had passed suddenly in his sleep, the spirit intelligence flowed. My sitter was emotional as it was his best friend and they were like brothers. Everything appeared to go well and after around forty-five minutes, I felt the energy change and it was time for me to end the sitting.

I mentioned to my sitter that I had finished now and he asked me if I could do one more thing. I agreed to try. "Can you give me his name, please? I have seen so many mediums but nobody gives me his name."

Names are difficult to receive, but not impossible either. I put the intention there but if I don't get it; I accept this is not how the spirit wishes to express themselves. Also, if you have already offered so much evidence, would you suddenly introduce yourself at the end? It was worth a try anyway and important to my sitter.

I asked my sitter to give me a few moments as I built my energy back and I put an intention to find his name. As I sat with my eyes shut, I was pleading for the name of this young man. There was nothing. I was asking for any help - but nothing dropped into my mind. All I could see were the insides of my eyelids. I let out an enormous sigh and said I'm so sorry but I can't find his name and just as I opened my eyes I saw a flash of an image which I thought was bizarre.

I told my sitter that I had to be added to the list of mediums who hadn't got his name. Perhaps it was unusual. Perhaps the expectation was too much. Maybe I tried too hard. I then mentioned how strange it was that I had a rapid image of something.

As I slowly opened my eyes, I saw the billboard poster of the film Rebel Without A Cause! I saw the picture of James Dean with a cigarette hanging from the side of his mouth. As I explained this, my sitter slid off the sofa and fell to his knees, weeping. When he recovered, he told me his friend's name was Dean James!

I had put my intention on finding the name of this young man in spirit. I was asking the wrong way. The moment I stopped trying with an expectation or a hope, my focus shifted to accepting nothing and in that moment, the spirit intelligence found the mind space to deliver.

Intention and focus are not a want and a concentrated effort, they are a state of being.

19

TRUSTING THE INTELLIGENCE

I am in awe of the architects of spirit intelligence - whoever they are. There has to be a way that this intelligence knows what's in the storehouses of human minds and how to bring the medium's attention to it. As sure as each of us is unique, the intelligence works with us. I don't know how they do it, but I know it is beyond my imagination. There may be theories, but life is one huge hypothesis, and I am left knowing what I know and reminding myself to trust.

It is when I don't trust that the mediumship struggles. Doubts creep in and confidence drops. As long as I am prepared to say I got it wrong, with no shame or ego, I am happy to do my work to the best of my ability. Trust is the key.

A most arduous task is communicating with spirit for someone you know, and are already familiar with their spirit loved ones. There is a constant mental battle of questions:

• Do I already know that, but forgot?

• Have I read this from them psychically, in previous encounters?

• What can I be sure I don't know?

I was demonstrating mediumship at the Arthur Findlay College a few years ago, when a 'familiar spirit' joined me on the platform. It was the husband of one of my students.

I had met him before from spirit in private sittings. I knew the events that led to his passing; I knew his personality, and I had spoken many times with the student socially, who had given me a lot of information about their life together.

This time, if he had something to communicate, it had to be information I was totally unaware of. I made it known to the student that her husband had joined me again. I publicly made it clear I knew a lot about him already, so I needed to focus on what he was about to say to her.

As I sensed his spirit close to me, I intended we had a journey where he could show me something I didn't or couldn't know. I took a few slow breaths to take myself into a better flow state.

An image appeared in my mind immediately, and he was sitting on top of the Alps. He had a small rucksack, a notebook, and pencil. This was understood by his wife so far. I needed more and suddenly I was seeing the world through his eyes.

I was looking at all the mountain peaks as if I was actually there. Their shapes and heights all signified something. In the notebook, he drew a musical stave. Each peak made a unique sound. My mind darted rapidly between the peaks, creating music. The best analogy I can offer is likened to the coloured lights in the film 'Close Encounters Of The Third Kind,' each playing a sequence of notes. Based upon the mountain peaks, I then observed him plot the notes on the hand drawn stave in the notebook.

In the next image he was at home playing the inspired mountain music on a piano and on the top of the page was her name.

I took another deep breath as I thought this sounded too fanciful, and I had probably imagined it all. I doubted myself for a moment. Then I remembered to trust and to let go of the fear of being wrong. So I spoke of the experience and what her husband had done for her.

It turned out it was all true. He had climbed the Alps, composed music inspired by the mountain peaks, dedicated it to her and also played it. Recently, she had been clearing out some boxes and found the original notebook. He wanted her to remember how much she meant to him. Music was both his passion and profession.

To get to the evidence and the intelligence of spirit, I had to let go of the fear of previous knowledge, fear of being wrong in front of an audience, fear of an unusual event being inaccurate. I had to give total trust to the spirit.

If we don't trust ourselves, or we doubt the spirit, or fear failure, we create a barrier that will prevent the communication of genuine spirit intelligence.

20

10 PIECES OF ADVICE I WOULD GIVE TO MY YOUNGER MEDIUM SELF

As your mediumship development progresses, there are several areas of focus which help with finding the intelligence of spirit. Mediumship is not the end game of spiritual development, but if you take this path in your life, a focus on your own personal development is vital.

As you learn and experience more, you will change and the change needs to be positive. To achieve the greatest intelligence from your spirituality and mediumship development, I have outlined a few areas which make a significant difference. You may already be doing them, but if not - they are here for your consideration.

1: Develop a regular practice for self and spirit.

Discipline, dedication and hard work are key components to mediumship.

Experiment with meditation techniques which quieten the mental chatter. When you find what works well for you, make it a regular activity.

Learn and grow your own spirit power. Exercises such as sitting in the power are excellent. There are many versions, so again, experiment with what works for you. Many are available freely on YouTube and websites, or you can purchase a personal copy from download music stores.

2: Know where the ideas originate from

Once you have established your regular practice of meditation and sitting in the power, you will be much clearer in your thoughts and where they originate. You will know if your mind was in a state of observation when something occurred spontaneously, or whether you controlled the thought that came to mind.

3: Be authentically you.

Whether or not you follow a path of mediumship, you are unique. If you try to emulate someone else's style, it won't work. If a spirit wishes to communicate with you, it is probable it is because you are the right medium for them to work with. Adopting the style of another medium will have you engaged in their techniques and not communicating with spirit. It's an unwelcome distraction and leads to poor communication.

Banish the idea that you are an imposter and embrace the seeker within you.

4: Get rid of pedestals

Always respect your teachers and express gratitude, but never worship them or use their name to attempt credibility. They are also still developing and sharing their wisdom and knowledge. Turning up in their class, no matter how many times, doesn't mean you improved your spirit communication or became a better human. Acknowledge their part in your journey, but never use their name to promote yourself or a product.

They have earned their reputation through hard work, and now it is time for you to establish your good name.

5: Objective analysis

Keep a journal of your spirit communications and write down anything that stood out as unusual, different, or just didn't work. Merging how you have worked and reflecting on it at a later date can lead to a greater understanding. Foster a critically kind approach in yourself. At the time of a sitting or demonstration, the adrenaline is high and the excitement of the occasion can lead you to overlook important clues to your progress.

After a while, write down any key points as if you were an observer of the sitting. This will help you gain new perspectives and guide you to areas that may need more focus.

With permission, record yourself, and after a few days listen to or watch the replay. Make notes on what had emotional and social intelligence and any aspects that you would like to improve on or discard in your work.

6: Describe your communication as you work

A lovely technique to work with is describing your experiences. Mediums can easily get into the habit of saying "they are telling me..." when in fact you saw an image, heard a sound or have a feeling, etc. When you present your communication as "I am being shown, I hear, I feel, I taste, I have a knowing" you accurately describe how you are communicating. When you do this, you are also educating the recipient or audience on how your spirit communication manifests. Vitally, you are teaching yourself, and you will gain confidence in knowing how you have been working.

7: Show up, support, and treat others the way you wish to be treated.

There are enough sceptics, armchair critics and the downright condescending opinions about spirit communication. Many reading this book will be working mediums or those on the path of mediumship. We understand how distracting and demoralising it can be at times.

Support is something I have advocated for many years. We need to build supportive networks. We must stop the competing and criticisms of other mediums. None of us appreciate it from the sceptics, but it is much worse when we propagate it ourselves.

If you see a medium struggling, remember it could be you next time. Offer the hand of friendship and show appreciation that they stepped up to the plate.

We can all play our part and when we hear someone being derogatory about another, we don't have to engage with it. Perhaps say something such as "I wonder if we can help them." It soon changes the tone of the critic.

8: Trust

At the front of the book is a quote 'Spirit is that which sees the truth of each moment, and does not cling to any conclusion.' One of the many reasons we don't trust ourselves is fear of failure. What happens in cases of the dreaded fear of failure is the medium plays safe with generalisations. It is unsatisfactory, misses the genuine message of spirt and feeds the sceptics.

If we trust the process, trust ourselves to do our best and trust the spirit intelligence, we are likely to be rewarded, if we have put in the work. Add an ingredient of doubt or playing safe, and so much is lost.

Ultimate trust requires that we overcome the fears and learn to accept when something hasn't worked out as planned. Sometimes, we get what what we need and not what we want.

When I look back over the years of engaging with spirit intelligence, I am proud that despite falling short on occasions; I got back up, learned more, studied more and prepared to fail again. Be bold and trust.

9: Practice the flow state

I wrote earlier that our greatest inspirations often arrive when in the flow state. Whether it is through meditation, art, music, writing or sitting for spirit, the flow state is your best friend for spirit intelligence.

If you can set aside time to get lost in a creative frame of mind, you are as close as possible to the spirit mind. In the spirit world, we do not exist with clocks, days, weeks, work agendas. Spirit is that in which we see the truth of each moment. The flow state induces the present moment and a timelessness that parallels the ways of the spirit.

10: Focus on the job and not your performance

The significance of working for spirit is that it is never about us. The focus is on the spirit intelligence and the recipient. Mediumship is the 'broker'. The moment we shift our focus to our performance or accuracy, we lose the intelligent connections that matter. It is easy to blame it on ego, yet sometimes is can be that too.

However, whether spirit communication takes place in a sitting or a public demonstration, focus is imperative.

In the public arena, there is an emphasis on good presentation. If this is your pathway, invest in some training in public presentation and public speaking. Once you have mastered the skills, they will become second nature, so you can truly place your focus on the intelligence of sprit.

GLOSSARY

1. Apports: objects that materialise in a seance room from elsewhere
2. Arthur Findlay College (AFC): A world renowned Spiritualist college of psychic sciences
3. Attunement: relates to a state of energetic spiritual harmony
4. Clairvoyance: Images in the mind
5. Clairaudience: Sounds, words or phrases in the mind
6. Clairsentience: Sensing information
7. Claircognisance: Sensing knowledge
8. Clairolfactrience: Sensing an aroma
9. Clairgustance: Sensing a taste
10. Discarnate: without a body

11. Ectoplasm: a substance exuded by the medium to create forms within physical mediumship
12. ESi - Emotional, Social, intelligence
13. Evidential medium: Someone who communicates with the deceased and provides evidence of their continued existence
14. Incarnate: with a physical body
15. Mental mediumship: mind to mind communication and subject to the influence of the mind of both parties. This is the most common form of mediumship
16. Objective clairvoyance: experiencing as if the vision is physically present
17. Physical mediumship: the phenomenon of spirit is objective and physical. It will be observed by all and not subject to the mind of either sitter of medium
18. Precognitive: having or giving foreknowledge of an event
19. Psychic medium: The psychic medium is someone who interprets the energy of a living being or earthly object and communicates the impressions received through their senses.

20. Psychic Readings: an intuitive reading of the energy relating to situations or personality traits etc.
21. Psychometry: Intuitively, reading the residual energy of objects.
22. Rappings: Tapping or knocking sounds purportedly made from a spirit, as a means of communication
23. Sitter: A person/client receiving a 'sitting' with an intuitive/psychic/evidential medium or present in a seance/circle
24. Sitting: a meeting between a medium and a sitter
25. Subjectively clairvoyant: experiencing the vision within the mind
26. Spirit guide - a spiritual archetype assigned only to you, to assist your spiritual progress

ABOUT THE AUTHOR

Helen DaVita is the Principal of Eagle Lodge Training and is also an approved training provider. She carries over 30 years of wisdom as an International spiritual teacher & inspirational speaker, world-renowned Intuitive, Arthur Findlay College Tutor/Course Organiser and sentient Animal Communicator. Helen is likewise a leading educator of being in altered states and trance mediumship.

Her 'Sitting In the Power' guided exercise has had over 1 million downloads and reached a global audience. It is freely available on her website and YouTube channel.

Helen's belief, is that we are all 'one' - one universe, one nature, one family and that spiritual development must be in harmony with the one family approach, to be authentic. Authenticity is found in a type of 'permaculture' of the spirit. Each aspect has a purpose, and it must not be divisive or create a separation. It must encompass nature, animals and energy. It is the way our ancient ancestors knew to survive and has no religion.

Printed in Great Britain
by Amazon

40578703R00088